BEGINNER'S SPANISH FOR ADULTS:

"Speak Spanish Rapidly: Master Language & Travel
Essentials: 2-in-1 Adult Guide" - BOOK 1

AUSTIN FULTZ

Contents

Introduction

¡Hola, amigos y amigas! I'm Austin, a fellow language enthusiast and your guide on this exciting journey into the Spanish-speaking world. My adventures through Latin America have not only taught me the language but also the profound beauty of its cultures. This book is my invitation to you to join in the exploration and discovery of Spanish.

Learning Spanish is a journey filled with challenges, immense rewards, and growth. Together, we'll uncover the nuances of the language and the cultures that enrich it, turning every possible obstacle into an opportunity for progress.

Remember: the path to fluency is a testament to our perseverance. This adventure is more than memorizing words; it's about connecting with others and embracing the journey with an open heart.

Anything truly worthwhile requires effort. So, as we embark on this journey together, let's make a pact to never give up on ourselves, on each other, or on the beautiful destinations that await us. After all, *"En la unión está la fuerza"* – in unity, there is strength.

Let this be our affirmation: We are boundless explorers of the world and the vast landscapes within us. Together, we will discover, grow, and, most importantly, thrive.

Book Breakdown:

- Embark on an exhilarating journey with **Book 1** as we plunge headfirst into the vibrant waters of the Spanish language! You're about to arm yourself with nifty words and phrases that are so practical that you'll start sprinkling them in conversations as if by magic. And fear not the challenge of pronunciation - we've got phonetic guides so spot-on you won't miss those audio clips one bit. But that's not all; we're taking a deep dive into the heart of Hispanic cultures. Prepare to navigate its nuances with the grace of a seasoned explorer. Each chapter is marked with keywords and common phrases, pronunciation keys, fill-in-the-blank worksheets, and lively dialogues straight from the daily lives of friends and family. It's not just learning; it's an adventure in every page-turn.
- **Book 2** cranks up the challenge, zeroing in on the backbone of Spanish communication: grammar. Brace yourself for a thrilling ride through past,

present, and future tense verbs, streamlined to the 22 most essential verbs for each tense. Yes, it's a brain workout that will demand your memory's A-game, but imagine the power at your fingertips when you master these verbal gems! Each chapter concludes with a fill-in-the-blank worksheet to reinforce your newfound skills. And here's a pro tip: transform those verbs into flashcards. Writing them down isn't just busywork; it's a brain-building, memory-maximizing strategy to supercharge your learning.

- As you go through these books, remember: practice makes perfect—and creative practice makes it fun. Talk to your dogs, cats, chickens, and pigs in Spanish. Who knows? One day, they might talk back. And if you ever doubt yourself, remember: *"The limits of my language are the limits of my world."* - Ludwig Wittgenstein. You've got this! Let's break down those limits and expand your world, one Spanish word at a time.

QUICK NOTE: The Spanish pronunciations In this book are broken down phonetically.

What does that mean? Phonetic English is like a unique code that shows how to say words. Each symbol stands for a specific sound, and it helps you say words correctly, even if they look tricky. You match the symbols with the sounds they represent and then practice saying the words aloud. It's all about listening, repeating, and getting the hang of it over time.

Before We Get Started: The Spanish Alphabet

Welcome to the Spanish alphabet, an essential foundation for your journey into the Spanish language! As an adult beginner, understanding the alphabet is your first step toward mastering pronunciation, spelling, and reading in Spanish. The Spanish alphabet is quite similar to the English one, with a few notable differences that we'll explore.

Here's a rundown of the Spanish alphabet with English phonetic pronunciations to help you get started:

1. **A** (a) – [ah]
2. **B** (be) – [beh]
3. **C** (ce) – [seh]
4. **D** (de) – [deh]
5. **E** (e) – [eh]
6. **F** (efe) – [eh•feh]
7. **G** (ge) – [heh] (before E, I) /geh/ (before A, O, U)
8. **H** (hache) – [ah•cheh] (silent)
9. **I** (i) – [ee]
10. **J** (jota) – [ho•tah]
11. **K** (ka) – [kah]
12. **L** (ele) – [eh•leh]
13. **M** (eme) – [eh•meh]
14. **N** (ene) – [eh•neh]
15. **Ñ** (eñe) – [eh•nyeh]
16. **O** (o) – [oh]
17. **P** (pe) – [peh]
18. **Q** (cu) – [koo]
19. **R** (ere) – [eh•reh] (soft) [erre] (rolled)

20. **S** (ese) – [eh•seh]
21. **T** (te) – [teh]
22. **U** (u) – [oo]
23. **V** (ve) – [beh] or [veh] (often pronounced the same as B) or [oo•veh]
24. **W** (doble ve) – [doh•bleh veh] or [doh•bleh oo] (less common, used in foreign words)
25. **X** (equis) – [eh•kees] (can vary based on the word)
26. **Y** (ye) – [yeh] or [ee gree•eh•gah] (used to be called "I griega")
27. **Z** (zeta) – [seh•tah]

Comparison to the English Alphabet:

- The Spanish alphabet contains 27 letters, including the unique "Ñ" not found in English.
- Pronunciation can vary between dialects, especially the letters "C," "Z," and "Y," as well as some syllables.
- The letter "H" is always silent in Spanish unless it is located between the letter "C" and a vowel, producing the sound "CH" (a little stronger than in English). For example, the word *"mucho"* (much) would be pronounced /moo-cho/.
- "V" and "B" have very similar pronunciations in many dialects, leading to minimal distinction between them in spoken language.
- "J" has a distinctive sound much stronger than the English "H."

Key Differences:

- The addition of "Ñ" introduces a unique sound ([ny]), enriching the language with words like "*niño*" (child).
- The distinction between the soft and rolled "R" sounds (as in "*pero*" vs. "*perro*") can alter meanings, a feature not present in English.
- Spanish pronunciation is more consistent and phonetic than English. Once you learn the sounds associated with each letter, you can correctly pronounce almost any word in Spanish.

Chapter One

In a bustling Madrid café, surrounded by the chatter of daily life, ordering a coffee becomes a bridge to a new world. The exchange is brief, but the connection is real. Armed with a few key phrases and an open heart, you find the courage to step into this vibrant tapestry of language and culture. This chapter is your gateway to those first crucial steps in Spanish, focusing on greetings, expressions of politeness, introducing yourself, and articulating everyday needs and feelings. It's about equipping you with the linguistic tools to navigate social situations, making every interaction an opportunity to learn and connect.

1.1 Getting Started with Spanish: Essential Greetings and Expressions

Greetings and Farewells

The cornerstone of any conversation, the ability to say hello and goodbye, sets the stage for positive interactions. In the Spanish-speaking world, these exchanges carry weight, often accompanied by a warmth that transcends the words themselves. For instance, *"Buenos días"* (Good morning) isn't just a greeting; it's an acknowledgment, a wish for the day ahead. Similarly, *"Hasta luego"* (See you later) promises future encounters, fostering a sense of community and belonging.

Understanding the context is crucial. *"Buenas noches"* can mean good evening and good night, but the situation determines its use. In greeting someone at 8 PM, you're wishing them a good evening. However, parting ways at the same hour, the phrase wishes them a good night. This duality highlights the importance of context in language, encouraging you to be observant and adaptive in your interactions.

KEYWORDS/PHRASES AND HOW TO PRONOUNCE THEM:

1. *Buenos días* [BWE•nos dEE•as] — (Good morning)
2. *Buenas tardes* [BWE•nas tAR•de] — (Good afternoon)
3. *Buenas noches* [BWE•nas NOH•ches] — (Good evening/Good night)
4. *Hola* [O•la] — (Hello)

5. *¿Cómo estás?* [KO•mo ehs•TAS] — (How are you? | Informal)

6. *¿Cómo está usted?* [KO•mo ehs•TA oos•TED] — (How are you? | Formal)

7. *Adiós* [ah•dee•OS] — (Goodbye)

8. *Hasta luego* [AH•sta LWE•go] — (See you later)

9. *Hasta mañana* [AH•sta ma•NYA•na] — (See you tomorrow)

10. *Nos vemos* [nos VE•mos] — (See you)

Politeness Essentials

Moving beyond greetings, the fabric of everyday conversation is woven with expressions of politeness. Phrases like *"por favor"* (please) and *"gracias"* (thank you) are not just markers of good manners but are pivotal in fostering mutual respect. They soften requests, making them more amicable, and express gratitude, acknowledging the effort of others.

Then there's *"disculpe"* (excuse me), a versatile tool in your linguistic arsenal. Whether navigating a crowded street or attracting a waiter's attention, *"disculpe"* is your go-to for initiating an interaction respectfully. It's about showing consideration for the space and time of others, a principle deeply rooted in Spanish-speaking cultures.

1. *Por favor* [por fa•VOR] — (Please)

2. *Gracias* [GRA•see•as] — (Thank you)

3. *Disculpe* [dis•KUL•pe] — (Excuse me)

4. *Lo siento* [lo SYEN-toh] — (I'm sorry | To apologize)

5. *Perdón* [per•DON] — (Sorry/Pardon | To apologize or when getting through)

6. *Con permiso* [kon per•MEE•so] — (Excuse me/Pardon me | When passing through or leaving)

7. *Mucho gusto* [MOO•cho GUS•to] — (Nice to meet you/

8. *De nada* [de NA•da] — (You're welcome)

9. *¿Podría ayudarme?* [po•DREE•a a•yoo•DAR•me] — (Can you help me?)

10. *Disculpa* [dis•KUL•pa] — (Sorry | Informal apology or to get attention)

Introducing Yourself and Others

Imagine you're at a local community event. The air buzzes with anticipation and faces around you are alight with smiles. Here, the ability to introduce yourself becomes a key that unlocks new friendships and opportunities. "*Me llamo...*" (My name is...) is the beginning, but sharing your name is just the first step. Asking "*¿Y tú, cómo te llamas?*" (And you, what's your name?) turns a monologue into a dialogue, an exchange.

Introducing others is equally important. "*Te presento a...*" (I introduce you to...) expands the conversation circle and demonstrates your role as a connector in social settings. It's about creating a network of interactions, each introduction a thread linking one person to another.

KEYWORDS/PHRASES AND HOW TO PRONOUNCE THEM:

1. *Me llamo...* [meh YAH•mo] — (My name is...)
2. *¿Y tú, cómo te llamas?* [ee TOO KOH•mo teh YAH•mas?] — (And you, what's your name?)
3. *Te presento a...* [teh preh•SEN•toh a...] — (I introduce you to...)
4. *Este es.../Esta es...* [EHS•te es.../EHS•ta es...] — (This is... | "*este*" for males; "*esta*" for females]
5. *Encantado/Encantada* [en•can•TAH•doh/en•can•TAH•dah] — (Pleased to meet you | "*encantado*" for males; "*encantada*" for females)
6. *Soy de...* [SOI de...] — (I am from...)
7. *Vivo en...* [VEE•voh en...] — (I live in...)
8. *Mi trabajo es...* [mee trah•BAH•ho es...] — (My job is...)
9. *Me gusta...* [meh GOOS•ta...] — (I like...)
10. *¿Cuál es tu hobby?/¿Qué te gusta hacer?* [KWAL es too hobby?/KEH te GOOS•ta ah•SER] — (What is your hobby?/What do you like to do?)

Common Expressions for Everyday Use

Everyday life is filled with moments that call for specific expressions. Whether you're expressing hunger, "*Tengo hambre*" (I'm hungry), or gratitude, "*Muchas gracias*" (Thank you so much), these phrases are your toolkit for navigating the day-to-day. They are more than words; they reflect needs, feelings, and reactions.

Consider the phrase *"Lo siento"* (I'm sorry). Its use goes beyond apologizing; it's an expression of empathy, a way to connect on a human level. Or *"¿Puedes ayudarme?"* (Can you help me?), a question that opens doors to assistance and interaction, signaling your willingness to learn and engage.

Each expression, from greetings to requests for help, lays down the foundational blocks of your Spanish journey. They are not just tools for communication but bridges to understanding and connecting you to Spanish-speaking people. Through them, you begin to navigate the complexities and joys of a new language, each word a step closer to a world of possibilities.

KEYWORDS/PHRASES AND HOW TO PRONOUNCE THEM:

1. *Tengo hambre* [TEN•go AHM•bre] — (I'm hungry)
2. *Muchas gracias* [MOO•chas grah•SIAS] — (Thank you very much)
3. *Lo siento* [loh SYEN•toh] — (I'm sorry)
4. *¿Puedes ayudarme?* [PWE•des ah•yoo•DAHR•meh] — (Can you help me?)
5. *¿Cómo estás?* [KOH•mo ehs•TAS] — (How are you?)
6. *Estoy bien, gracias* [es•TOI byen, GRAH•see•as] — (I'm well, thank you)
7. *¿Cuánto cuesta?* [kwan•TOH kwes•TAH?] — (How much does it cost?)
8. *No entiendo* [NOH en•TYEN•doh] — (I don't understand)
9. *¿Dónde está el baño?* [DOHN•de ehs•TAH el BAH•nyo?] — (Where is the bathroom?)

10. *Necesito ayuda* [neh•seh•SEE•toh ah•YOO•dah] —
    (I need help)

Chapter 1.1 Common Spanish phrases

1. *Buenos días, ¿cómo estás?* [BWE•nos DEE•ahs,
   KOH•mo ehs•TAHS?] — (Good morning; how are
   you?)
2. *Buenas tardes, me llamo Juan.* [BWE•nas THAR•des,
   meh YAH•mo hwan] — (Good afternoon; my name
   is Juan.)
3. *Buenas noches y hasta mañana.* [BWE•nas
   NOH•ches ee HAS•ta ma•NYA•nah] — (Good
   evening, and see you tomorrow.)
4. *Hola, mucho gusto en conocerte.* [O•lah, MOO•cho
   GOOS•toh en KOH•no•ser•teh] — (Hello, nice to
   meet you.)
5. *Adiós, nos vemos pronto.* [ah•dee•OS, nos VEH•mos
   PRON•to.] — (Goodbye, see you soon.)
6. *Disculpe, ¿podría ayudarme?* [dees•KOOL•pe,
   po•DREE•a a•yoo•DAR•me?] — (Excuse me,
   could you help me?)
7. *Lo siento, estoy un poco perdido.* [lo SYEN•to, es•TOI
   oon PO•ko per•DEE•do.] — (I'm sorry, I'm a bit
   lost.)
8. *Perdón, ¿dónde está el baño?* [per•DON, DON•de
   es•TAH el BAH•nyo?] — (Sorry, where is the
   bathroom?)
9. *Estoy bien, gracias. ¿Y tú?* [es•TOI byen,
   GRAH•see•as. ee TOO?] — (I'm well, thank you.
   And you?)

10. **Tengo hambre, ¿vamos a comer?** [TEN•go AHM•breh, VAH•mos ah ko•MER?] — (I'm hungry, shall we go to eat?)

Chapter 1.1 Worksheet

1) Fill in the blanks with the correct Spanish greetings, farewells, and other expressions from the list provided. This exercise will help you practice and reinforce some basics of Spanish communication. Good luck!

Example: _____ días (Good morning) -> Buenos días

Reference List:

- Hola
- Adiós
- Buenas noches
- Hasta luego
- Mucho gusto
- ¿Cómo estás?
- Bien gracias, ¿y tú?
- Nos vemos
- Buenas tardes
- Encantado/a
- Hasta mañana

_____ *Hello*)

_____ (tardes (*Good afternoon*)

_____ noches (*Good evening/Good night*)

Hasta _____ (*See you later*)

_____ gusto (*Nice to meet you*)

¿_____ estás? (*How are you?*)

_____ gracias, ¿y

_____ ? (*Fine, thanks, and you?*)

_____ vemos (*See you*)

_____ mañana (*See you tomorrow*)

Encantado/a (Pleased to meet you) - Use this when you are

_____ .

2) **Dialogue:** Let's dive into an authentic exchange featuring greetings and expressions you will likely encounter in a Spanish-speaking setting.

Alex: *Hola, soy Alex. ¿Y tú?*
[O•la, soy Alex. ee TOO?]
(Hello, I'm Alex. And you?)

Jamie: *Hola, soy Jamie, de Nueva York.*
[O•la, soy Jamie, de NWE•va York.]
(Hello, I'm Jamie, from New York.)

Alex: *¡Qué interesante! ¿Te gusta aquí?*
[KEH in•te•re•SAN•te! te GOOS•ta a•KEY?]
(How interesting! Do you like it here?)

Jamie: *Sí, mucho. Es muy diferente a Nueva York.*
[SEE, moo•cho. es MOO•y di•fe•REN•te a NWE•va York.]
(Yes, a lot. It's very different from New York.)

Alex: *Me imagino. Bueno, ¿nos vemos luego?*
[me ee•ma•HEE•no. BWE•no, nos VEH•mos LWE•go?]
(I can imagine. Well, shall we see each other again?)

Jamie: *Sí, ¡hasta luego!*
[SEE, AHS•ta LWE•go!]
Yes, see you later!

Alex: *Adiós.*
[ah•dee•OS.]
Goodbye.

1.2 Numbers, Days, and Time: Scheduling Your Life in Spanish

Imagine planning a get-together with new friends you've made in a Spanish-speaking community. You want to set the date, decide on the time and discuss what you'll do. This scenario isn't just about socializing; it's a practical exercise in applying your Spanish skills to real-life situations. So, how do you go about it?

Counting in Spanish

First up, numbers. They're everywhere, from prices at the market to street numbers and, yes, setting dates. Starting from *uno* (one) to *diez* (ten) lays the groundwork, but soon you'll find yourself comfortably moving up to *cien* (one hundred) and beyond, up to *mil* (one thousand). Imagine you're at a local market, eyeing a piece of art. The price? *Setecientos cincuenta* (seven hundred and fifty). The ability to understand and use numbers not only helps you navigate shopping but also in bargaining, telling time, and, of course, exchanging phone numbers.

A useful tip? Practice numbers in context. When you see prices while shopping or planning your budget, challenge yourself to think in Spanish. It's not just about memorization; it's about making numbers a part of your daily thought process.

KEYWORDS/PHRASES AND HOW TO PRONOUNCE THEM:

1. *Uno* [OO•no] — (One)
2. *Dos* [DOS] — (Two)
3. *Tres* [TRES] — (Three)
4. *Cuatro* [KWAH•tro] — (Four)
5. *Cinco* [SEEN•ko] — (Five)
6. *Seis* [SEYS] — (Six)
7. *Siete* [SYEH•te] — (Seven)

8. *Ocho* [O•cho] — (Eight)
9. *Nueve* [NWEH•ve] — (Nine)
10. *Diez* [DYEHZ] — (Ten)

- *Veinte* [VEYN•te] — (Twenty)
- *Treinta* [TREYN•ta] — (Thirty)
- *Cuarenta* [kwa•REN•ta] — (Forty)
- *Cincuenta* [seen•KWEN•ta] — (Fifty)
- *Sesenta* [se•SEN•ta] — (Sixty)
- *Setenta* [se•TEN•ta] — (Seventy)
- *Ochenta* [o•CHEN•ta] — (Eighty)
- *Noventa* [no•VEN•ta] — (Ninety)
- *Cien* [SYEN] — (One hundred)
- *Mil* [MEEL] — (One thousand)

Days of the Week and Months

Now, let's talk about days and months, the backbone of any plan. From *lunes* (Monday) to *domingo* (Sunday), knowing these allows you to schedule activities, make appointments, and join in on local events. And then, of course, there are the months, from *enero* (January) to *diciembre* (December), which are crucial for planning ahead or reflecting on past experiences.

Incorporate these into your routine. For instance, start your day by saying, "*Hoy es miércoles, trece de septiembre*" (Today is Wednesday, September 13). They will cement your knowledge and make you more comfortable discussing dates and plans in Spanish.

KEYWORDS/PHRASES AND HOW TO PRONOUNCE THEM:

Days of the Week

1. *Lunes* [LOO•nes] — (Monday)
2. *Martes* [MAR•tes] — (Tuesday)
3. *Miércoles* [MYER•koh•les] — (Wednesday)
4. *Jueves* [HWEH•ves] — (Thursday)
5. *Viernes* [VYER•nes] — (Friday)
6. *Sábado* [SAH•bah•doh] — (Saturday)
7. *Domingo* [do•MEEN•goh] — (Sunday)

Months of the Year

1. *Enero* [EH•ne•ro] — (January)
2. *Febrero* [feh•BREH•ro] — (February)
3. *Marzo* [MAR•zo] — (March)
4. *Abril* [a•BRIL] — (April)
5. *Mayo* [MAH•yo] — (May)
6. *Junio* [HOO•nyo] — (June)
7. *Julio* [HOO•lyo] — (July)
8. *Agosto* [a•GOS•to] — (August)
9. *Septiembre* [sep•TYEM•breh] — (September)
10. *Octubre* [ok•TOO•breh] — (October)
11. *Noviembre* [no•VYEM•breh] — (November)
12. *Diciembre* [dee•SYEM•breh] — (December)

Telling Time

When you're coordinating when to meet, telling time in Spanish becomes your next hurdle. The 24-hour clock is commonly used, so understanding the difference between, say, "*Son las tres*" (It's 3 PM) and "*Son las quince*" (It's 15:00) is critical. Also, phrases like "*¿A qué hora...?*" (At what time...?) become part of your planning toolkit, allowing you to quickly ask and inform about schedules.

A fun exercise is to switch your digital devices to display time in the 24-hour format and in Spanish. It's a small change, but checking the time becomes a mini Spanish lesson each time you go about your day.

Time can also be stated by using a 12-hour format and clarifying if you're speaking of *de la mañana* (in the morning), *de la tarde* (in the afternoon) or *de la noche* (at night).

KEYWORDS/PHRASES AND HOW TO PRONOUNCE THEM:

1. *¿Qué hora es?* [KEH O•rah ehs?] — (What time is it?)
2. *Es la una* [ehs lah OO•nah] — (It's one o'clock | used only for 1:00).
3. *Son las...* [son LAHS] — (It's... | used for times other than 1:00, e.g., "*Son las dos*" for 2:00).
4. *Y cuarto* [ee KWAR•toh] — (Quarter past | e.g., "*Son las tres y cuarto*" for 3:15).
5. *Menos cuarto* [MEH•nos KWAR•toh] — (Quarter to | e.g., "*Son las cuatro menos cuarto*" for 3:45).

6. *Y media* (ee MEH•dyah) — (Half past | e.g., "*Son las dos y media*" for 2:30).
7. *De la mañana* (deh lah mah•YAH•nah) — (In the morning | AM).
8. *De la tarde* (deh lah TAR•deh) — (In the afternoon | PM, afternoon until evening).
9. *De la noche* (deh lah NOH•cheh) — (In the evening/night | PM, generally after 6 PM).
10. *En punto* (en POON•toh) — (On the dot | e.g., "*Son las cinco en punto*" for 5:00 sharp).

Date Formats and Important Holidays

Now, about those dates. The format follows the day-month-year sequence, quite the opposite of what some might be used to. So, the 4th of July would be written as "*4 de julio.*" Understanding this format is essential, not just for setting personal appointments but also for understanding local events and holidays.

Speaking of holidays, familiarizing yourself with the significant ones of the country you're at, like "*Día de los Muertos*" (Day of the Dead) or "*Navidad*" (Christmas), offers a peek into the cultural richness of the Spanish-speaking world. It's not just about marking these days on your calendar; it's about understanding their significance, the associated traditions and how you can participate or respectfully observe these celebrations.

A Spanish calendar marked with these essential dates not only serves as a practical tool for planning but also immerses you in the cultural aspects of the language. You learn when to celebrate and why these moments are cherished, adding layers to your understanding and appreciation of the culture.

Through these topics, from numbers to holidays, you're not just learning Spanish; you're integrating it into the fabric of your daily life. It's about making the language a tool for living, not just a subject to study. So, next time you plan a gathering or navigate your schedule, remember these aren't just exercises in memorization. They're your steps toward living a life intertwined with a new language and culture, making every day an opportunity to learn, connect, and grow.

KEYWORDS/PHRASES AND HOW TO PRONOUNCE THEM:

Date Formats

1. Día/Mes/Año [DEE•ah/mehs/AH•nyo] — (Day-Month-Year, e.g., "*4 de julio de 2024*" (July 4, 2024).)

2. El primero de... [el PREE•meh•roh deh...] — (The first of..., 2 e.g., "*El primero de enero*" (January 1st).)

Essential Holidays and How to Pronounce Them

3. Día de los Muertos [DEE•ah deh los MWEHR•tos] — (Day of the Dead | celebrated on November 1st and 2nd to honor deceased loved ones]

4. Navidad [nah•vee•DAHD] — (Christmas | celebrated on

December 25th or the night of December 24th in some Hispanic countries.)

5. *Año Nuevo* [AH•nyo NWEH•vo] — New Year's Day, January 1st.

6. *Día de la Independencia* [DEE•ah deh lah een•deh•pen•DEN•syah] — (Independence Day | varies by country, e.g., September 16th in Mexico.)

7. *Semana Santa* [seh•MAH•nah SAHN•tah] — (The dates of Holy Week | the week before Easter, vary.)

8. *Día del Trabajo* [DEE•ah del trah•BAH•ho] — (Labor Day | May 1st in most Spanish-speaking countries.)

9. *Día de la Raza* [DEE•ah deh lah RAH•sah] — (Columbus Day/Indigenous Peoples' Day | October 12th.)

10. *Día de los Reyes Magos* [DEE•ah deh los REH•yes MAH•gos] — (Three Kings Day/Epiphany | celebrated on January 6th.)

Additional Notes

11. *Fiestas Patrias* [FYEHS•tahs PAH•tree•as] — (National holidays specific to each Spanish-speaking country, celebrating their independence or other significant national events.)

12. *Carnaval* [kar•nah•VAHL] (Carnival | celebrated in the days before Lent, with dates varying each year.)

Chapter 1.2 Common Spanish Phrases

1. *Hoy es lunes y tengo una reunión a las diez.* [oy es LOO•nes ee TEN•go OO•na reh•oo•nee•ON ah las DEYHZ] — (Today is Monday, and I have a meeting at ten.)

2. *El sábado vamos al cine a las ocho de la noche.* [el SAH•bah•doh VAH•mos ahl SEE•neh ah las O•cho deh lah NOH•cheh] — (On Saturday, we're going to the cinema at eight in the evening.)

3. *Mi cumpleaños es el veinte de julio.* [mee koom•pleh•AH•nyos es el veh•YN•teh deh HOO•lyo] — (My birthday is on the twentieth of July.)

4. *¿Qué hora es? Son las cuatro y media de la tarde.* [keh OR-ah ehs? son las KWAH•tro ee MEH•dyah deh lah TAR•deh] — (What time is it? It's four-thirty in the afternoon.)

5. *Necesito comprar mil huevos para la Semana Santa.* [neh•seh•SEE•toh kom•PRAR MEEL WEH•vos PAH•rah lah seh•MAH•nah SAHN•tah] — (I need to buy one thousand eggs for Holy Week.)

6. *El Día de los Muertos celebramos a nuestros antepasados.* [el DEE•ah deh los MWER•tos seh•leh•BRAH•mos ah noo•ES•tros ahn•teh•pah•SAH•dos] — (On the Day of the Dead, we celebrate our ancestors.)

7. *Navidad es mi fiesta favorita en diciembre.* [nah•vee•DAHD es mee FYES•tah fah•voh•REE•tah en dee•SYEM•breh] — (Christmas is my favorite holiday in December.)

8. *Vivo en una casa con cuatro habitaciones.* [VEE•voh en OO•nah KAH•sah kon KWAH•tro ah•bee•tah•see•OH•nes] — (I live in a house with four rooms.)

9. *¿Cuánto cuesta el boleto? Cincuenta pesos.* [KWAHN•toh KWES•tah el boh•LEH•toh? seen•KWEN•tah PEH•sos] — (How much does the ticket cost? Fifty pesos.)

10. *Año Nuevo es el primero de enero.* [AH•nyo NWEH•vo es el pree•MEH•roh deh eh•NEH•ro] — (New Year's Day is on the first of January.)

Chapter 1.2 Worksheet:

Counting in Spanish

1) **Fill in the blanks** with the correct Spanish numbers from 1 to 10.

Uno, dos, tres, _____, cinco, seis, siete, _____, nueve, diez.

Days of the Week

Complete the days of the week in Spanish, starting with Monday.

Lunes, martes, _____, jueves, _____, sábado, domingo.

Months of the Year

Fill in the missing months in Spanish.

Enero, febrero, marzo, _____, mayo,

_____, julio,

_____, septiembre,

_____, noviembre, diciembre.

Telling Time

Translate the following times into Spanish.

- It's 3 PM — "Son las

  _____

  horas."
- At what time? — "¿A qué

  _____?"
- It's 15:00 — "Son las

  _____

  horas."

Date Formats

- In Spanish, the date format follows the sequence of

  _____,

  _____ and

  _____ (day-month-year).
- Convert the date 'July 4th' into Spanish date format:

  _____ de _____ .
- Write the date 'December 25th' in Spanish,
  following the correct format: _____ de

  _____ .
- How would you write '1st of January' in Spanish?

  _____ de _____ .

Important Holidays

- "*Día de los Muertos*" is celebrated on
  _____ and
  _____ -
  _____ (write the dates).
- Translate and write the date for 'Christmas' in
  Spanish: _____
- When is "*Día de la Independencia de México*"? Write the
  date in Spanish: _____
- "*Semana Santa*" (Holy Week) falls around the time of
  _____(*month*).
  When exactly it occurs can vary each year.
- The day celebrating 'Columbus Day' in Spanish-
  speaking countries is often known as
  _____ and occurs on
  _____ (*date*).

Dialogue: below, you'll pick up vital Spanish phrases for scheduling and discussing dates. Focus on days, numbers, time, and a notable holiday. Use this conversation to practice making plans in Spanish.

Carlos: *Hola Elena, ¿quieres salir este sábado?*
[O•la eh•LEH•na, KYEH•res sa•LEER EHS•te SA•ba•do?]
(Hello Elena, do you want to go out this Saturday?)

Elena: *Hola Carlos. Sí, ¿a qué hora?*
[O•la KAR•los. SEE, a KEH O•ra?]
(Hello Carlos. Yes, at what time?)

Carlos: *A las diez, ¿te parece bien?*
[a las DYEHZ, te pa•REH•se byen?]
(At ten, does that sound good to you?)

Elena: *Perfecto. ¿Vamos al parque?*
[per•FEK•to. VAH•mos al PAR•ke?]
(Perfect. Shall we go to the park?)

Carlos: *Sí, y luego podemos comer algo.*
[SEE, ee LWE•go po•DEH•mos ko•MER AHL•go.]
(Yes, and then we can eat something.)

Elena: *¡Genial! También, el 16 de septiembre es importante, ¿verdad?*
[he•NYAL! tam•BYEN, el dee•e•SEYS de sep•TYEM•bre es im•por•TAN•te, ver•DAHD?]
(Great! Also, September 16th is important, right?)

Carlos: *Sí, es el Día de la Independencia. Podemos planear algo especial.*
[SEE, es el DEE•a de la in•de•pen•DEN•sia. po•DEH•mos pla•NEAR AL•go es•pe•SYAL.]
(Yes, it's Independence Day. We can plan something special.)

Elena: *Me encanta la idea. Hasta el sábado entonces.*
[meh en•KAN•ta la ee•DEH•a. HAS•ta el SA•ba•do en•TON•ces.]
(I love the idea. See you then on Saturday.)

Carlos: *Hasta luego, Elena.*
[HAS•ta LWE•go, eh•LEH•na.]

(See you later, Elena.)

Elena: *Adiós, Carlos.*
[ah•dee•OS, KAR•los.]
(Goodbye, Carlos.)

1.3 Food and Dining: Order at a Restaurant with Confidence

Navigating the culinary landscape of a Spanish-speaking country is akin to stepping into a living, breathing cookbook where each page reveals new flavors, aromas, and traditions. It's an adventure where language is pivotal in unlocking local dining experiences. Now, let's explore how to order at a restaurant confidently, decode a Spanish menu, and understand the cultural nuances that make dining out a key part of the Hispanic world's charm.

Menu Navigation

Deciphering a Spanish menu starts with recognizing the structure: *Entradas* (appetizers), *platos principales* (main courses), *postres* (desserts), and *bebidas* (drinks). This familiarity means you can dive straight into what interests you most. For those with dietary preferences or restrictions, keywords such as *vegetariano* (vegetarian), *sin gluten* (gluten-free), or *alérgico* (allergic to) become your allies. It helps to know the names of everyday dishes and ingredients, but don't hesitate to ask your server for recommendations: "*¿Qué recomienda?*" Their insight often leads to discovering dishes that become the highlight of your meal.

Menus in Spanish-speaking countries are an invitation to explore regional cuisines. For instance, *ceviche* in Peru, *tapas* in Spain, or *tacos* in Mexico, each item tells a story of local flavors and traditions. When unfamiliar terms arise, view them as an opportunity to expand your vocabulary and palate. A quick note or photo of new words adds to your culinary and linguistic repertoire, turning every meal into a learning experience.

KEYWORDS/PHRASES AND HOW TO PRONOUNCE THEM:

1. *Entradas* [en•TRAH•das] — (Appetizers)
2. *Platos principales* [PLAH•tos prin•see•PAH•les] — (Main courses)
3. *Postres* [POS•tres] — (Desserts)
4. *Bebidas* [be•BEE•das] — (Drinks)
5. *Vegetariano* [ve•he•ta•RYA•no] — (Vegetarian)
6. *Sin gluten* [seen GLOO•ten] — (Gluten-free)
7. *Alérgico a* [a•LEHR•hi•ko a] — (Allergic to)
8. *¿Qué recomienda?* [KEH reh•ko•MYEN•dah?] — (What do you recommend? | Use this to ask your server for their recommendations.)
9. *¿Tiene opciones vegetarianas?* [TYEH•neh op•see•OH•nes ve•he•ta•RIAH•nas?] — (Do you have vegetarian options? | Essential for those with dietary preferences or restrictions.)
10. *¿Este plato contiene gluten?* [ES•teh PLAH•to kon•TYEH•neh GLOO•ten?] — (Does this dish contain gluten? | Important for guests with gluten sensitivity.)

11. *Ceviche* [seh•VEE•cheh] — A seafood dish marinated in citrus juices, widespread in coastal regions of Latin America.
12. *Tapas* (TAH•pas) — Small Spanish appetizers or snacks.
13. *Tacos* (TAH•kos) — A traditional Mexican dish with a small, hand-sized corn or wheat tortilla topped with a filling.

Ordering Food and Drinks

Placing your order confidently is about more than just stating what you'd like. It's about engaging in a brief exchange that enhances your dining experience. Start with "*Me gustaría...*" (I would like...) or "*Quisiera...*" (I would want...) to express your choices politely. If you're curious about a dish, don't hesitate to ask, "*¿Qué lleva el...?*" (What's in the...?). This helps you make informed choices and sparks a connection with those who prepare and serve your food.

Making special requests is an exercise in clarity and politeness. "*Sin*" (without) and "*con más*" (with more) are handy prepositions for tweaking dishes to your liking. Remember, patience and a smile are your best companions here, as accommodating custom orders might take more time and explanation.

As for drinks, whether it's *"una cerveza"* (a beer), *"un vaso de agua"* (a glass of water) or *"una copa de vino"* (a glass of wine), specifying your beverage choice is a good practice. If you're dining out with others, a collective *"Para beber, nos gustaría..."* (For drinks, we would like...) streamlines the ordering process, making it smoother for you and your server.

KEYWORDS/PHRASES AND HOW TO PRONOUNCE THEM:

1. *Me gustaría...* [meh goos•tah•REE•ah] — (I would like...)
2. *Quisiera...* [kee•SYEH•rah] — (I would want...)
3. *¿Qué lleva el...?* [KEH YEH•vah el...?] — (What's in the...?)
4. *Sin...* [seen...] — (Without...)
5. *Con más...* [kon MAHS...] — (With more...)
6. *Una cerveza* [OO•nah ser•VEH•zah] — (A beer)
7. *Un vaso de agua* [oon VAH•so deh AH•gwah] — (A glass of water)
8. *Una copa de vino* [OO•nah KO•pah deh VEE•no] — (A glass of wine)
9. *Para beber, nos gustaría...* [PAH•rah be•BER, nos goos•tah•REE•ah...] — (For drinks, we would like...)
10. *¿Puede ser sin...?* [PWEH•deh ser seen...?] — (Can it be without...? | useful for making special requests or mentioning dietary restrictions.)
11. *¿Tienen algún plato vegetariano?* [TYEH•nen AHL•goon PLAH•toh ve•he•ta•REE•ah•no?] — (Do you have any vegetarian dishes?)

12. *¿Podría traerme...?* [po•DREE•ah tra•ER•meh...?] —
    (Could you bring me...? | this is a polite way to
    request something.)
13. *La cuenta, por favor.* [lah KWEN•tah, por fah•VOR]
    — (The bill, please.| essential for concluding your
    meal.)

Paying and Tipping

When settling the bill, *"La cuenta, por favor"* (The bill, please)
is your key phrase. In many Spanish-speaking regions, it's
customary for the bill not to be brought to your table until
requested, a practice that respects the leisurely pace at
which meals are often enjoyed. As for tipping, practices vary
by country and setting. In some places, a service charge is
included in the bill (*servicio incluido*), while in others, leaving
an additional 10-15% of the total is expected for good service.
Familiarizing yourself with local customs regarding tipping
prevents awkward moments and ensures you're showing
appreciation appropriately.

Carrying small bills and coins makes it easier to leave tips,
especially in casual dining settings where splitting the bill
might be more complex. If you're unsure, a discrete question
to a local or a quick online search before your meal can
guide you on the customary practice.

KEYWORDS/PHRASES AND HOW TO PRONOUNCE
THEM:

1. *La cuenta, por favor* [lah KWEN•tah, por fah•VOR]
   — (The bill, please.)

2. *Servicio incluido* [ser•VEE•syo in•kloo•EE•doh] —
   (Service included.)

3. *¿Está incluido el servicio?* [ehs•TAH in•kloo•EE•doh
   el ser•VEE•syo?] — (Is service included?)

4. *Propina* [proh•PEE•nah] — (Tip.)

5. *Sin servicio incluido* [seen ser•VEE•syo
   in•kloo•EE•doh] — (Without service included.)

6. *Dejar una propina* [deh•HAR OO•nah
   proh•PEE•nah] — (To leave a tip.)

7. *¿Cuánto debo dejar de propina?* [KWAN•toh
   DEH•boh deh•HAR de proh•PEE•nah?] — (How
   much should I leave for a tip?)

8. *Pago en efectivo* [PAH•go en eh•fek•TEE•voh] —
   (Cash payment.)

9. *¿Puedo pagar con tarjeta?* [PWE•doh pa•GAR kon
   tar•HEH•tah?] — (Can I pay with a card?)

10. *Dividir la cuenta* [dee•vee•DEER lah KWEN•tah]
    — (Split the bill.)

11. *Cambio* [KAM•byoh] — (Change | money).

12. *¿Pueden cambiar un billete grande?* [PWE•den
    kam•byar oon bee•YEH•teh GRAHN•deh?] —
    (Can you change a large bill?)

13. *¿Aceptan efectivo?* [ah•sep•TAN eh•fek•TEE•voh?]
    — (Do you accept cash?)

14. *¿Aceptan dólares?* [ah•sep•TAN DOH•lah•res?] —
    (Do you accept dollars?)

Cultural Tips for Dining Out

The experience of dining out extends beyond the flavors on your plate; it's a window into the cultural fabric of a region. As you can expect, customs will vary according to the country, region and/or social setting you're at. For instance, meal-times often occur later than what many non-natives might be accustomed to. Lunch, the main meal of the day in many Spanish-speaking countries, might not start until 2 PM or later, while dinner can stretch well into the night, beginning at 9 PM or even later.

Understanding this rhythm is crucial; it informs not just when you eat but how meals are approached. Dining is a leisurely affair, a time for conversation, savoring each dish, and simply enjoying the moment. Rushing through a meal misunderstands the essence of these cultures' approach to dining.

Moreover, sharing dishes is common in many places, with *tapas* in Spain being a prime example. This practice not only allows you to try a variety of flavors but also reflects the communal aspect of meals. It's about sharing not just food but experiences, stories and laughter.

Lastly, remember that every meal allows you to practice your Spanish in a real-world setting. From ordering to interacting with servers and fellow diners, each moment is a step towards fluency, filled with the potential for delightful discoveries and connections. So, next time you scan a menu in a bustling eatery, embrace the experience with confidence and curiosity. After all, dining out is about nourishing the body, feeding the soul and expanding the mind, one Spanish word at a time.

More About Tapas and How to Order and Share Them with Friends and Family:

Tapas are a cornerstone of Spanish cuisine, offering a diverse array of small dishes to be shared among friends or family. From Spain, tapas range from simple items like olives and cheese to elaborate dishes such as *patatas bravas* (spicy potatoes) and *gambas al ajillo* (garlic shrimp). The tradition of tapas started as a simple, practical gesture: bars would cover (or *"tapar"* in Spanish) drinks with a small plate of food to protect them from flies, eventually becoming a social dining experience.

How to Order and Share Tapas:

1. **Start Small:** Order a few tapas for the table. It's common to start with 2-3 tapas for a group of two and adjust based on the group's size and appetite.
2. **Mix and Match:** Select a variety of tapas to enjoy a range of flavors. Include both cold (like cheeses and cured meats) and hot dishes (like croquettes or fried seafood).
3. **Sharing is Key:** Tapas are meant to be shared. Place them in the center of the table so everyone can try a bit of everything.
4. **Order as You Go:** Order a few dishes at a time instead of ordering everything at once. This way,

you can gauge your hunger and try more dishes if desired.

5. **Communicate with Your Server:** Feel free to ask for recommendations. Servers can guide you to the house specialties or explain dishes you need to familiarize yourself with.

6. **Enjoy the Experience:** Tapas dining is as much about the social experience as the food. Savor the dishes, the company, and the conversation.

Embracing tapas culture means embracing a leisurely, sociable and diverse way of eating. It's an invitation to explore a variety of dishes, engage in lively conversation, and enjoy the pleasure of sharing food.

Chapter 1.3 Common Spanish Phrases

1. *Para beber, quisiera una copa de vino.* [PAH•rah be•BER, kee•SYEH•rah OO•nah KO•pah deh VEE•no] — (For a drink, I would like a glass of wine.)

2. *¿Tiene opciones vegetarianas?* [TYEH•neh op•see•OH•nes ve•he•ta•RIAH•nas?] — (Do you have vegetarian options?)

3. *Me gustaría probar el ceviche.* [meh goos•tah•REE•ah pro•BAR el seh•VEE•cheh] — (I would like to try the ceviche.)

4. *¿Este plato contiene gluten?* [ES•teh PLAH•to kon•TYEH•neh GLOO•ten?] — (Does this dish contain gluten?)

5. *Para empezar, nos gustarían unas tapas.* [PAH•rah em•peh•SAR, nos goos•tah•REE•an OO•nas TAH•pas] — (To start, we would like some tapas.)

6. *¿Qué recomienda como plato principal?* [KEH reh•ko•MYEN•dah KOH•mo PLAH•to prin•si•PAHL?] — (What do you recommend as a main course?)

7. *Sin gluten, por favor.* [seen GLOO•ten, por fah•VOR] — (Gluten-free, please.)

8. *La cuenta, por favor.* [lah KWEN•tah, por fah•VOR] — (The bill, please.)

9. *¿Está incluido el servicio?* [ehs•TAH in•kloo•EE•doh el ser•VEE•syo?] — (Is service included?)

10. *Quisiera pagar con tarjeta.* [kee•SYEH•rah pa•GAR kon tar•HEH•tah] — (I would like to pay with a card.)

Chapter 1.3 Worksheet

1) Fill in the blanks with the appropriate Spanish words or phrases based on the context provided. This worksheet is designed to help you practice common Spanish vocabulary and phrases used in menu navigation, ordering food and drinks, paying, tipping, and understanding cultural norms in dining settings.

Menu Navigation

- When looking at a menu, you'll find the

_____ (*appetizers*),

_____(*main courses*),

_____(desserts), and

_____(drinks).

Ordering Food and Drinks

- To express your desire for a dish politely, you might start with

  "_____"

  (I would like...) or

  "_____"

  (I would want...).
- If curious about the ingredients in a dish, ask

  "_____"

  (What's in the...?).

Paying and Tipping

- To request the bill, you say

  "_____,

  por favor" (The bill, please).
- If you want to know if cash is accepted, you might ask

  "_____"

  (Do you accept cash?) and for using dollars specifically,

  "_____"

  (Do you accept dollars?).

Cultural Tips for Dining Out

- Understanding that
  "_____"
  (*service charge*) might already be included in your
  bill is essential, as tipping customs can vary.

Using what we've learned, engage in a family conversation
with a server, focusing on ordering food at a restaurant.

Family Members: Juan (Father), María (Mother), Sofía
(Daughter), Alejandro (Son)

Juan: *¿Podemos ver el menú?*
[po•DEH•mos ver el me•NOO?]
(Can we see the menu?)

Camarero (Waiter): *Claro, aquí tienen. ¿Algo de beber?*
[KLA•ro, a•KEE tee•EH•nen. AL•go de be•BER?]
(Of course, here you are. Something to drink?)

María: Un agua mineral, por favor.
[oon AHa•gwa mi•ne•RAL, por fa•VOR.]
(A mineral water, please.)

Sofía: *Yo quiero jugo de naranja.*
[yo KYE•ro HOO•go de na•RAN•ha.]
(I want orange juice.)

Alejandro: *Quisiera croquetas de jamón.*
[kee•SYE•ra kro•KEH•tas de ha•MON.]

(I would like ham croquettes.)

Juan: *¿Qué recomienda?*
[KEH re•ko•MYEN•da?]
(What do you recommend?)

Camarero: *El lomo saltado es popular.*
[ehl LOH•mo sal•TAH•do es po•pu•LAR.]
(The lomo saltado is popular.)

María: *Dos lomos saltados, por favor.*
[dos LOH•mos sal•TAH•dos, por fa•VOR.]
(Two lomo saltados, please.)

Juan: *¿Aceptan tarjeta?*
[a•SEP•tan tar•HE•ta?]
(Do you accept cards?)

Camarero: *Aceptamos ambas, efectivo es mejor.*
[a•sep•TAH•mos AM•bas, e•fek•TEE•vo es me•HOR.]
(We accept both, cash is better.)

Sofia: *¿Podemos pedir postre después?*
[Po•DE•mos pe•DEER POS•tre des•pu•ES?]
(Can we order dessert later?)

Camarero: *Tenemos buenos postres.*
[te•NE•mos BWE•nos POS•tres.]
(We have good desserts.)

Alejandro: *¿Cuánto es la propina?*
[KWAN•to es la pro•PEE•na?]
(How much is the tip?)

Juan: *Normalmente, el 10%.*
[nor•MAL•men•te, el DYEHZ porSYEN•to.]
(Normally, 10%.)

María: *Al final, la cuenta, por favor.*
[ahl fi•NAL, la KWEN•ta, por fa•VOR.]
(At the end, the bill, please.)

Camarero: *Disfruten.*
[dis•FROO•ten.]
(Enjoy.)

1.4 Shopping in Spanish: From Groceries to Souvenirs

Navigating a Spanish-speaking country's lively markets and bustling stores can be an adventure. Each interaction and transaction is a step deeper into the heart of local life. Knowing the terminology of shopping is vital to genuinely engaging. It's about more than just transactions; it's about connecting, discovering, and even enjoying the art of the deal.

Basic Shopping Vocabulary

Before you set foot in a market or a boutique, familiarizing yourself with the names of typical shops can transform your experience. *"Panadería"* means bakery, *"carnicería"* means butcher shop, and "*mercado*" means market; each term opens up a new avenue of exploration. Then there's "*farmacia*" for pharmacy, "*librería*" means bookstore, and "*tienda de ropa*" means clothing store, guiding you to the places you need or want to visit.

Products and transactions also have their own vocabulary. Terms like "*rebaja*" (sale), "*descuento*" (discount), and "*oferta*" (offer) are music to any shopper's ears, signaling opportunities to save. "*Efectivo*" (cash), "*tarjeta*" (card), and "*cambio*" (change) are part of the checkout dialogue, smoothing the path from selection to purchase.

KEYWORDS/PHRASES AND HOW TO PRONOUNCE THEM:

1. *Panadería* [pah•nah•deh•REE•ah] — (Bakery)
2. *Carnicería* [kar•nee•seh•REE•ah] — (Butcher shop)
3. *Mercado* [mer•CA•do] — (Market)
4. *Farmacia* [phar•MAH•see•ah] — (Pharmacy)
5. *Librería* [lee•breh•REE•ah] — (Bookstore)
6. *Tienda de ropa* [TYEN•dah deh ROH•pah] — (Clothing store)
7. *Rebaja* [reh•BAH•hah] — (Sale)
8. *Descuento* [des•KWEN•to] — (Discount)
9. *Oferta* [oh•FEHR•tah] — (Offer)
10. *Efectivo* [eh•fehk•TEE•vo] — (Cash)
11. *Tarjeta* [tar•HEH•tah] — (Card)
12. *Cambio* [KAHM•bee•oh] — (Change)

Additional Phrases for Shopping

- *¿Cuánto cuesta?* [KWAN•toh KWES•tah?] — (How much does it cost?)
- *¿Tiene esto en otra talla?* [TYEH•neh EHS•toh en O•trah TAH•yah?] — (Do you have this in another size?)
- *¿Puedo pagar con tarjeta?* [PWEH•doh pah•GAR kon tar•HEH•tah?] — (Can I pay with a card?)
- *¿Dónde está el probador?* [DON•deh es•TAH el pro•bah•DOR?] — (Where is the fitting room?)
- *Necesito un recibo* [ne-•seh•SEE•toh oon reh•SEE•boh] — (I need a receipt)

Asking for Prices and Sizes

Once you're in the store, you will need to ask about prices and sizes. "*¿Cuánto cuesta?*" (How much does it cost?) is your go-to question for price inquiries. For clothing and shoes, knowing how to ask for your size, "*¿Tiene esto en talla...?*" (Do you have this in size...?) or "*¿Tiene esto en número...?*" (Do you have this in a number...?) for shoes, which ensures you find the perfect fit.

Negotiation is another aspect of the shopping experience, especially in markets. Phrases like "*¿Puede darme un mejor precio?*" (Can you give me a better price?) Show not only your interest but also your respect for the bargaining culture. It's a dance of words, where each party seeks value in the exchange.

KEYWORDS/PHRASES AND HOW TO PRONOUNCE THEM:

1. *¿Cuánto cuesta?* [KWAN•toh KWES•tah?] — (How much does it cost?)

2. *¿Tiene esto en talla...?* [TYEH•neh EHS•toh en TAH•yah...?] — (Do you have this in size...?)

3. *¿Tiene esto en número...?* [TYEH•neh EHS•toh en NOO•meh•roh...?] — (Do you have this in number...? | for shoes)

4. *¿Puede darme un mejor precio?* [PWEH•deh DAR•meh oon meh•HOR PREH•see•oh?] — (Can you give me a better price?)

5. *¿Esto está en oferta?* [EHS•toh es•TAH en oh•FEHR•tah?] — (Is this on sale?)

6. *¿Puedo probar esto?* [PWEH•doh proh•BAR EHS•toh?] — (Can I try this on?)

7. *¿Cuál es su precio final?* [KWAL es soo PREH•see•oh fee•NAL?] — (What is your final price?)

8. *¿Aceptan tarjetas?* [ah•SEHP•tan tar•HEH•tahs?] — (Do you accept cards?)

9. *¿Tienen algún descuento?* [TYEH•nen al•GOON des•KWEN•toh?] — (Do you have any discount?)

10. *¿Puedo pagar en efectivo?* [PWEH•doh pah•GAR en eh•fehk•TEE•voh?] — (Can I pay in cash?)

11. *¿Tienen esto en otro color?* [TYEH•nen EHS•toh en OH•troh koh•LOR?] — (Do you have this in another color?)

12. *¿Cómo me queda?* [KOH•mo meh KEH•dah?] — (How does it fit me?)

Additional Phrases for Shopping Interaction

- *Estoy buscando...* [es•tTOI boos•KAHN•doh...] —
  (I'm looking for...)
- *Es para un regalo* [ehs PAH•rah oon reh•GAH•loh]
  — (It's for a gift)
- *¿Puede envolverlo para regalo?* [PWEH•deh
  en•vol•VER•loh PAH•rah reh•GAH•loh?] — (Can
  you gift-wrap it?)
- *¿Cuál es la política de devolución?* [KWAL es lah
  po•LEE•tee•kah deh deh•vo•loo•see•OHN?] —
  (What is the return policy?)

Understanding Labels and Receipts

Reading labels and receipts is akin to decoding a cultural
and nutritional map. Labels tell you not just about ingredients, "*ingredientes*," but also about origins, "*origen*," and expiration dates, "*fecha de caducidad*." They offer insights into the
local diet, preferences, and regulatory standards. On the
other hand, receipts, or "*recibos*," detail your purchases,
taxes, ("*impuestos*,") and sometimes even suggest how to
prepare or use the product. Though seemingly mundane,
this information enriches your understanding of local shopping practices and consumer rights.

Navigating labels and receipts is a practical vocabulary-
building exercise for non-native speakers. It turns every
shopping trip into an interactive language lesson, where
each label or receipt is a flashcard in disguise. This hands-on

approach broadens your linguistic skills and deepens your immersion in the local culture.

INSERT KEYWORDS/PHRASES AND HOW TO PRONOUNCE THEM:

1. *Ingredientes* [een•gre•DYEN•tes] — (Ingredients)
2. *Origen* [o•REE•hen] — (Origin)
3. *Fecha de caducidad* [FEH•cha de ka•du•si•DAHD] — (Expiration date)
4. *Recibos* [re•SEE•bos] — (Receipts)
5. *Impuestos* [eem•PWES•tos] – (Taxes)
6. *Precio total* [PRE•syo to•TAL] — (Total price)
7. *Cantidad* [kan•ti•DAHD] — (Quantity)
8. *Peso neto* [PEH•so NEH•to] — (Net weight)
9. *Información nutricional* [een•for•ma•SYON nu•tri•syo•NAL] — (Nutritional information)
10. *Instrucciones de uso* [eens•truc•SYO•nes de OO•so] — (Instructions for use)
11. *Descuento* [des•KWEN•to] — (Discount)
12. *IVA | Impuesto sobre el Valor Añadido* [EE•VA | eem•PWES•to SOH•bre el va•LOR ah•ña•DEE•do] — (VAT | Value Added Tax)
13. *Número de lote* [NOO•me•ro de LOH•te] — (Batch number)
14. *Fecha de elaboración* [FEH•cha de e•la•bo•ra•SYON] — (Manufacture date)
15. *Conserve en lugar fresco y seco* [kon•SER•ve en LOO•gar FRES•ko y SEH•ko] — (Keep in a cool and dry place)

Additional Phrases for Understanding Labels and Receipts

- *Hecho en* [EH•cho en] — (Made in)
- *Caduca en* [kah•DOO•kah en] — (Expires on)
- *Sin gluten* [seen GLOO•ten] — (Gluten-free)
- *Alto en fibra* [AHL•to en FEE•bra] — (High in fiber)
- *Bajo en grasa* [BAH•ho en GRA•sa] — (Low in fat)

Cultural Insights into Shopping

Shopping in Hispanic regions is not just about acquiring goods; it's about embracing the rhythm and rituals of local life. For instance, *siesta* time, a cherished tradition in many parts of Spain and Latin America influences shopping hours. Many shops close in the early afternoon, only to reopen later, blending commerce with the culture's value on rest and family time.

While common in markets, bargaining is an art form that reflects the social and economic fabric of the community. It's not just about getting the best price but about interaction, respect, and humor. Knowing when and how to engage in this practice shows your appreciation for local customs.

Popular items vary significantly from one region to another, offering a window into the community's heart. In Mexico, you might search for artisanal *"alebrijes"* (colorful, fantastical creatures), while in Spain, an *"abanico"* (hand fan) might catch your eye. These items are not just souvenirs; they're tangible connections to the place and its people.

With its vocabulary, negotiations and insights, shopping is a microcosm of the broader cultural experience. Each purchase and interaction weaves you deeper into the social fabric, transforming you from an outsider to a participant in the daily dance of commerce and community.

KEYWORDS/PHRASES AND HOW TO PRONOUNCE THEM:

1. *Siesta* [see•EHS•tah] — (Siesta)
2. *Horario comercial* [oh•RAH•ryo koh•mer•SYAL] — (Business hours)
3. *Regateo* [reh•ga•TEH•oh] — (Bargaining)
4. *Mercado artesanal* [mer•KAH•do ar•te•sa•NAL] — (Craft market)
5. *Cierre a mediodía* [CYE•rre a me•dyo•DEE•ah] — (Midday closing)
6. *Trato personalizado* [TRA•to per•so•na•li•ZAH•do] — (Personalized service)
7. *Productos locales* [pro•DOOK•tos lo•KAH•les] — (Local products)
8. *Alebrijes* [ah•le•BREE•hes] — (Alebrijes | Artisanal colorful creatures from Mexico)
9. *Abanico* [ah•ba•NEE•ko] — (Fan | Hand fan, often associated with Spain)
10. *Cultura de la negociación* [kul•TOO•ra de la ne•go•si•a•SYON] — (Negotiation culture)
11. *Tiempo con la familia* [TYEM•po kon la fa•MEE•lya] — (Family time)
12. *Valorar el descanso* [va•lo•RAR el des•KAN•so] — (To value rest)

13. *Interacción social* [een•ter•rak•SYON so•SYAL] — (Social interaction)

14. *Respeto mutuo* [res•PEH•to MOO•tuo] — (Mutual respect)

15. *Humor en el trato* [OO•mor en el TRA•to] — (Humor in the interaction)

Additional Cultural Insights

- *Compra de proximidad* [KOM•pra de pro•xi•mi•DAHD] — (Local shopping | Supporting local vendors)
- *Producto artesanal* [pro•DOOC•to ar•te•sa•NAL] — (Handcrafted product)
- *Tradición y modernidad* [tra•di•SYON y mo•der•ni•DAHD] — (Tradition and modernity)
- *Experiencia de compra* [ex•pe•RYEN•cia de KOM•pra] — (Shopping experience)
- *Sabores locales* [sa•BO•res lo•KAH•les] — (Local flavors)

Chapter 1.4 Common Spanish Phrases

1. *En la panadería venden el mejor pan.* [en lah pah•nah•deh•REE•ah VEN•den el meh•HOR pan] — (They sell the best bread at the bakery.)

2. *Compré carne fresca en la carnicería.* [KOM•preh KAR•neh FRES•kah en lah kar•nee•seh•REE•ah] — (I bought fresh meat at the butcher shop.)

3. *Vamos al mercado por verduras.* [VAH•mos al

mer•CAH•doh por ver•DOO•rahs] — (Let's go to
the market for vegetables.)

4. *Necesito medicina de la farmacia.* [neh•seh•SEE•toh
meh•dee•SEE•nah deh lah
phar•MAHmah•see•ah] — (I need medicine from
the pharmacy.)

5. *Busco un libro en la librería.* [BOOS•koh oon
LEE•broh en lah lee•breh•REE•ah] — (I'm looking
for a book at the bookstore.)

6. *¿Cuánto cuesta esta camisa en la tienda de ropa?*
[KWAN•toh KWES•tah EHS•tah kah•MEE•sah en
lah TYEN•dah deh ROH•pah?] — (How much does
this shirt cost at the clothing store?)

7. *Hay una rebaja en las bebidas hoy.* [eye OO•nah
reh•BAH•hah en las beh•BEE•dahs oy] — (There's
a sale on drinks today.)

8. *¿Puedo pagar con tarjeta o solo efectivo?* [PWEH•doh
pah•GAR kon tar•HEH•tah oh SOH•loh
eh•fehk•TEE•voh?] — (Can I pay with a card or
only cash?)

9. *¿Tiene esto en otra talla?* [TYEH•neh EHS•toh en
OH•trah TAH•yah?] — (Do you have this in
another size?)

10. *Quisiera un descuento en este.* [kee•SYEH•rah oon
des•KWEN•toh en EHS•teh] — (I would like a
discount on this.)

Chapter 1.4 Worksheet

1) Write down the appropriate Spanish words or phrases
based on the context provided. Topics include basic shop-

ping vocabulary, asking for prices and sizes, understanding labels and receipts, and cultural insights into shopping.

Basic Shopping Vocabulary

- Bakery

  _____

- Butcher Shop

  _____

- Market

  _____

- Pharmacy

  _____

- Clothing Store

  _____

Asking for Prices and Sizes

- ¿Cuánto

  _____?

  (*How much does it cost?*)

- ¿Tiene esto en
  _____? (*Do you
  have this in size...?*)
- ¿Puede darme un
  _____ precio? (*Can
  you give me a better price?*)

Understanding Labels and Receipts

- Fecha de _____
  (*Expiration date*)
- Infor _____
  nutricional (*Nutritional information*)
- Número de _____
  (*Batch number*)

Cultural Insights into Shopping

- Afternoon rest impacting business hours

  _____

- Craft market

  _____

- Local product

  _____

2) **Dialogue:** In this simplified shopping conversation, readers can expect to encounter basic Spanish vocabulary related to shopping, including asking for prices and sizes and understanding labels.

- Focus on the interaction patterns and critical phrases that facilitate a smooth shopping experience in a Spanish-speaking environment.

John: *Hola, ¿hay rebajas en camisetas?*
[O•la, eye reh•BAH•has en ka•mee•SEH•tas?]
(Hello, are there sales on T-shirts?)

María: *Sí, con 20% de descuento.*
[see, kon VEYN•teh por SYEN•toh deh des•KWEN•toh.]
(Yes, with a 20% discount.)

John: *¿Tiene en talla M?*
[TYEH•neh en TAH•ya M?]
(Do you have it in size M?)

María: *Aquí tiene.*
[ah•KEE TYEH•neh.]
(Here you have it.)

John: *¿Cuánto cuesta esto?*
[KWAN•toh KWES•tah EHS•toh?]
(How much is this?)

María: *15 euros.*
[KEEN•seh EH•oo•rohs.]
(15 euros.)

John: *Lo llevaré. ¿Aceptan tarjeta?*
[lo yeh•va•REH. Ah•SEP•tan tar•HEH•tah?]
(I'll take it. Do you accept card?)

María: *Sí, aquí su recibo.*
[SEE, ah•KEE soo reh•SEE•boh.]
(Yes, here's your receipt.)

John: *Gracias, ¿y una panadería cerca?*
[GRAH•syahs, ee OO•nah pah•nah•deh•REE•ah
SER•kah?]
(Thank you, and a bakery nearby?)

María: *Al salir, a la izquierda.*
[al sah•LEER, ah la eez•KYER•dah.]
(When you leave, to the left.)

John: *Gracias por todo.*
[GRAH•syahs por TOH•doh.]
(Thanks for everything.)

María: *De nada, disfruta.*
[deh NAH•dah, dees•FROO•tah.]
(You're welcome, enjoy.)

1.5 Finding Your Way: Directions and Transportation Essentials

Navigating a Hispanic country's streets and transportation systems may feel challenging. Each step, turn, and gesture communicates direction, intent, and connection. In this vibrant setting, knowing how to ask for and give directions, understand public transportation terminology, and maneuver through airports and stations becomes your dance guide, ensuring you move through the landscape with ease and confidence.

Asking for and Giving Directions

When you find yourself at the crossroads of a bustling city or a quaint village, the ability to inquire about directions is invaluable. Starting with "*¿Dónde está...?*" (Where is...?) or "*¿Cómo llego a...?*" (How do I get to...?) opens up a path to exploration. Responses often include "*a la derecha*" (to the right), "*a la izquierda*" (to the left), "*todo recto*" (straight ahead), or "*cerca de*" (near), guiding you step by step towards your destination.

On the flip side, giving directions allows you to share knowledge and connect with others on their path. Using landmarks, "*al lado de*" (next to), "*enfrente de*" (in front of) or "*detrás de*" (behind), helps paint a clearer picture for the seeker. Remember, gestures add to words, turning the exchange into a shared experience bridging language and understanding.

KEYWORDS/PHRASES AND HOW TO PRONOUNCE
THEM:

1. *¿Dónde está...?* [DON•deh es•TAH] — (Where is...?)
2. *¿Cómo llego a...?* [KOH•moh YE•go ah...?] — (How
   do I get to...?)
3. *A la derecha* [ah lah deh•REH•chah] — (To the
   right)
4. *A la izquierda* [ah lah iz•KYER•dah] — (To the left)
5. *Todo recto* [TOH•doh REK•toh] — (Straight ahead)
6. *Cerca de* [SER•kah deh] — (Near)
7. *Al lado de* [al LAH•doh deh] — (Next to)
8. *Enfrente de* [en•FREN•teh deh] — (In front of)
9. *Detrás de* [deh•TRAHS deh] — (Behind)
10. *Hasta* [AHS•tah] — (Until)

Public Transportation Vocabulary

The pulse of public transportation offers a glimpse into the
daily rhythm of local life. Here, buses (*"autobuses"*), trains
(*"trenes"*), and taxis (*"taxis"*) become your vessels through the
urban landscape. Knowing how to inquire about schedules,
"¿Cuándo sale el próximo autobús?" (When does the next bus
leave?), or ticket prices, *"¿Cuánto cuesta un billete para el tren?"*
(How much is a ticket for the train?) ensures you navigate
this network with ease.

For those venturing further, long-distance buses and trains
connect you to new adventures. Phrases like *"¿Este autobús va
a...?"* (Does this bus go to...?) or *"Quiero un billete de ida y vuelta"* (I

want a round-trip ticket) are keys to unlocking these journeys. Each ride, each ticket, weaves you deeper into the fabric of the place, offering windows into landscapes and lives in motion.

KEYWORDS/PHRASES AND HOW TO PRONOUNCE THEM:

1. *Autobuses* [ow•toh•BOO•sehs] — (Buses)
2. *Trenes* [TREH•nehs] — (Trains)
3. *Taxis* [TAK•sees] — (Taxis)
4. *¿Cuándo sale el próximo autobús?* [KWAN•doh SAH•leh ehl PROHK•see•moh ow•toh•BOOS?] — (When does the next bus leave?)
5. *¿Cuánto cuesta un billete para el tren?* [KWAN•toh KWES•tah oon bee•YEH•teh PAH•rah el tren?] — (How much is a ticket for the train?)
6. *¿Este autobús va a...?* [EHS•teh ow•toh•BOOS vah ah...?] — (Does this bus go to...?)
7. *Quiero un billete de ida y vuelta* [KYEH•roh oon bee•YEH•teh deh EE•dah ee WELL•tah] — (I want a round-trip ticket)
8. *Horario* [o•RAH•ree•oh] — (Schedule)
9. *Parada* [pah•RAH•dah] — (Stop | bus/train)
10. *Estación* [ehs•tah•SYOHN] — (Station)
11. *Billete* [bee•YEH•teh] — (Ticket)
12. *Tarifa* [tah•REE•fah] — (Fare)
13. *Plataforma* [plah•tah•FOR•mah] — (Platform)
14. *Vagón* [vah•GOHN] — (Carriage)

Navigating Airports and Stations

Airports and train stations are hubs of activity and gateways to discovery. From the moment you step in, understanding signs like "*Salidas*" (Departures), "*Llegadas*" (Arrivals), "*Recogida de equipaje*" (Baggage claim), and "*Control de pasaportes*" (Passport control) guide you through the maze of procedures and checkpoints. Inquiring about boarding gates or platforms, "*¿De qué puerta sale mi vuelo?*" (From which gate does my flight leave?) or "*¿En qué andén está el tren?*" (On which platform is the train?) becomes second nature, ensuring you're on the right path to your next adventure.

For those moments of waiting, "*sala de espera*" (waiting room) offers a pause, a breath during transit. Here, observing, listening, and engaging with fellow travelers adds layers to your journey, offering stories and connections that enrich the experience beyond the destination.

KEYWORDS/PHRASES AND HOW TO PRONOUNCE THEM:

1. *Salidas* [sah•LEE•dahs] — (Departures)
2. *Llegadas* [yeh•GAH•dahs] — (Arrivals)
3. *Recogida de equipaje* [reh•coh•HEE•dah deh eh•kee•PAH•heh] — (Baggage claim)
4. *Control de pasaportes* [kohn•TROL deh pah•sah•POR•tes] — (Passport control)
5. *¿De qué puerta sale mi vuelo?* [deh KEH PWER•tah SAH•leh mee VWEH•loh?] — (From which gate does my flight leave?)

6. *¿En qué andén está el tren?* [en KEH ahn•DEN
   ehs•TAH el tren?] — (On which platform is the
   train?)

7. *Sala de espera* [SAH•lah deh ehs•PEH•rah] —
   (Waiting room)

8. *Taquilla* [tah•KEE•yah] — (Ticket counter)

9. *Puerta de embarque* [PWER•tah deh em•BAR•keh]
   — (Boarding gate)

10. *Facturación* [fahk•too•ra•SYON] — (Check-in)

11. *Seguridad* [seh•goo•ree•DAHD] — (Security)

12. *Aduana* [ah•DWAH•nah] — (Customs)

13. *Información* [een•for•mah•SYON] — (Information)

14. *Zona de recogida de equipajes* [SOH•nah deh
    reh•coh•HEE•dah deh eh•kee•PAH•hehs] —
    (Baggage reclaim area)

Cultural Norms for Getting Around

The way people move and interact during transit speaks
volumes about local culture. In many Spanish-speaking
countries, greeting drivers with a *"Buenos días"* or *"Buenas
tardes"* reflects respect and acknowledgment, a small gesture
fostering community.

While only sometimes expected, tipping is appreciated for
exceptional service, especially in taxis. A simple rounding
up of the fare or a small additional amount reflects gratitude
and respect for the driver's work, strengthening the bond
between guest and host.

Purchasing tickets often requires patience, a nod to the slower pace of life embraced in many regions. Whether at a kiosk, "*taquilla*," or through a machine, "*máquina expendedora*," the process is an exercise in presence. It involves taking the time to ensure your passage is secured and honoring the journey ahead.

For many, bicycles ("*bicicletas*") offer a closer connection to the streets and sights. Bike-sharing programs in cities invite you to pedal through history, culture and daily life, blending in with the local flow. Inquiring about rental stations, "*¿Dónde puedo alquilar una bicicleta?*" (Where can I rent a bicycle?) opens up a path of exploration powered by your pace and curiosity.

However, it is recommended you do a little online research about these matters before your arrival at the city.

Navigating the landscapes of Spanish-speaking countries by foot, wheel or wing is an integral part of the language learning experience. Each step and ride is a dialogue with the environment, a dance of directions and discovery. In these moments of transit, you find yourself not just moving through but becoming part of the world around you, each destination a new verse in your ongoing conversation with the language and its speakers.

KEYWORDS/PHRASES AND HOW TO PRONOUNCE THEM:

I. *Buenos días* [BWE•nos DEE•ahs] — (Good morning)

2. *Buenas tardes* [BWE•nas TAR•des] — (Good afternoon)
3. *Propina* [proh•PEE•nah] — (Tip)
4. *Taquilla* [tah•KEE•yah] — (Ticket booth)
5. *Máquina expendedora* [MAH•kee•nah eks•pen•deh•DOH•rah] — (Ticket machine)
6. *Bicicletas* [bee•see•KLE•tas] — (Bicycles)
7. *¿Dónde puedo alquilar una bicicleta?* [DON•deh PWEH•doh al•kee•LAR OO•nah bee•see•KLE•tah?] — (Where can I rent a bicycle?)
8. *Saludo al conductor* [sah•LOO•doh al kon•dook•TOR] — (Greeting the driver)
9. *Agradecimiento al bajar* [ah•grah•deh•see•mee•EN•toh al bah•HAR] — (Thanking when getting off)
10. *Paciencia en la compra* [pah•see•EN•see•ah en lah KOM•prah] — (Patience in purchasing)
11. *Programas de compartición de bicicletas* [proh•GRA•mas de kom•par•tee•SYON de bee•see•KLE•tas] — (Bike-sharing programs)
12. *Integración con la comunidad* [een•teh•grah•SYON kon lah ko•moo•neeDAHD] — (Integration with the community)

Chapter 1.5 Common Spanish Phrases

1. *¿Dónde está la estación de autobuses?* [DON•deh es•TAH lah ehs•tah•SYOHN deh ow•toh•BOO•sehs?] — (Where is the bus station?)
2. *¿Cómo llego a la estación de trenes?* [KOH•moh

YEH•go ah lah ehs•tah•SYOHN deh treh•nehs?] —
(How do I get to the train station?)

3. *¿Cuánto cuesta un billete para el tren a Madrid?*
[KWAN•toh KWES•tah oon bee•YEH•teh PAH•ra
el tren ah mah•DREED?] — (How much is a ticket
for the train to Madrid?)

4. *¿Este autobús va al centro de la ciudad?* [EHS•teh
ow•toh•BOOS vah al SEN•troh deh lah
see•oo•DAHD?] — (Does this bus go to the city
center?)

5. *Quiero un billete de ida y vuelta para Barcelona.*
[KYEH•roh oon bee•YEH•teh deh EE•dah ee
VWELL•tah PAH•ra bar•the•LOH•nah.] — (I want
a round-trip ticket to Barcelona.)

6. *¿A qué hora es el próximo tren?* [ah KEH O•rah ehs el
PROK•see•moh tren?] — (What time is the next
train?)

7. *¿Dónde puedo alquilar una bicicleta cerca de la
estación?* [DON•deh PWEH•doh al•kee•LAR
OO•nah bee•see•KLEH•tah SER•kah deh lah
ehs•tah•SYOHN?] — (Where can I rent a bicycle
near the station?)

8. *¿De qué plataforma sale el tren a Sevilla?* [deh KEH
plah•tah•FOR•mah SAH•leh el tren ah
seh•VEE•yah?] — (From which platform does the
train to Seville leave?)

9. *¿Dónde está la parada del taxi?* [DON•deh es•TAH
lah pah•RAH•dah del taxi?] — (Where is the taxi
stop?)

10. *¿Cuándo sale el próximo autobús a la playa?*
[KWAN•doh SAH•leh el PROK•see•moh

ow•toh•BOOS ah lah PLA•yah?] — (When does the next bus to the beach leave?)

Chapter 1.5 Worksheet

1) Fill in the blanks with the correct Spanish words or phrases to complete the sentences.

Asking and Giving Directions

- ¿ _____ está el baño? (*Where is the bathroom?*)
- Vas todo _____ y luego giras a la derecha. (*Go straight ahead and then turn right.*)
- ¿Cómo _____ a la estación de tren? (*How do I get to the train station?*)
- Está a la _____ después de la plaza. (*It's on the left after the square.*)
- Puedes tomar el autobús número 5 o caminar unos 10 minutos, está

  _____ de aquí. (*You can take bus number 5 or walk about 10 minutes, it's near here.*)

Public Transportation Vocabulary

- Necesito comprar un

  _____ para el autobús. (*I need to buy a ticket for the bus.*)
- ¿Cuándo sale el próximo

_____? (*When does the next bus leave?*)

- ¿Este autobús va a

  _____? (*Does this bus go to...?*)

- Quiero un billete de

  _____ y vuelta. (*I want a round-trip ticket.*)

- La _____ de trenes está al otro lado de la ciudad. (*The train station is on the other side of the city.*)

Navigating Airports and Stations

- Debo pasar por el

  _____ de seguridad antes de ir a mi puerta de embarque. (*I must go through the security checkpoint before going to my boarding gate.*)

- Mi vuelo sale de la

  _____ B. (*My flight leaves from gate B.*)

- ¿Dónde está la _____ de recogida de equipaje? (*Where is the baggage claim area?*)

- Tengo que hacer

  _____ en el mostrador. (*I have to check in at the counter.*)

- Busco la sala de

  _____ para esperar

mi vuelo. (*I'm looking for the waiting room to wait for my flight.*)

Cultural Norms for Getting Around

- Es común saludar al conductor con un '
  _____ días' al subir al
  autobús. (*It's common to greet the driver with a 'Good
  morning' when boarding the bus.*)
- Al tomar un taxi, es cortés
  _____ la tarifa si el
  servicio fue excepcional. (*When taking a taxi, it's
  polite to round up the fare if the service was exceptional.*)
- La paciencia es clave al comprar boletos en una
  _____ . (*Patience is key
  when buying tickets at a kiosk.*)
- Alquilar una _____
  puede ser una excelente manera de explorar la
  ciudad. (*Renting a bicycle can be an excellent way to
  explore the city.*)
- Caminar es una forma popular de
  _____ y experimentar
  la cultura local. (*Walking is a popular way to get
  around and experience the local culture.*)

2) **Dialogue:** This conversation focuses on key phrases for navigating transportation and asking for directions in Spanish.

John: ¿Dónde está la estación de autobuses?
[DON•de es•TAH la es•ta•SYON de ow•to•BOO•ses?]

(Where is the bus station?)

Elena: Ve derecho y luego a la derecha. Está cerca de la plaza.
[VEH de•RE•cho ee LWE•go a la de•RE•cha. ehs•TAH SER•ka de la PLA•za.]
(Go straight and then right. It's near the square.)

John: ¿Necesito comprar un billete primero?
[neh•se•SEE•to kom•PRAR un bee•YEH•te pri•MEH•ro?]
(Do I need to buy a ticket first?)

Elena: Sí, compra el billete en la taquilla.
[SEE, KOM•pra el bee•YEH•te en la ta•KEE•ya.]
(Yes, buy the ticket at the ticket office.)

John: ¿Y los taxis?
[ee los taxis?]
(And the taxis?)

Elena: Hay taxis cerca del supermercado.
[eye taxis SER•ka del su•per•mer•KAH•do.]
(There are taxis near the supermarket.)

John: Gracias por tu ayuda.
[GRAH•syas por tu a•YOO•da.]
(Thank you for your help.)

Elena: De nada. Buen día.
[de NAH•da. BWEN DEE•a.]
(You're welcome. Have a good day.)

1.6 Health and Emergencies: Navigating Medical Conversations

A specific vocabulary becomes indispensable when navigating healthcare or facing emergencies in Spanish-speaking places. Not only does it facilitate communication, but it also ensures you can express concerns accurately and seek the necessary assistance. This segment aims to cover the linguistic tools required for such situations and insights into healthcare interactions' cultural nuances.

Basic Health Vocabulary

Acquiring terms related to common illnesses and symptoms paves the way for describing how you feel to a healthcare professional. Words like *"fiebre"* (fever), *"tos"* (cough) and *"dolor"* (pain) followed by the body part (e.g., *"dolor de cabeza"* for headache) are foundational. Understanding these terms allows you to convey your symptoms succinctly, aiding in quicker diagnosis and treatment. Similarly, familiarizing oneself with the names of body parts enhances communication, making examinations or describing discomfort more straightforward.

When it comes to medical facilities, knowing the difference between "hospital" (hospital), "clínica" (clinic), and "farmacia" (pharmacy) is crucial. While a hospital provides many services, a clinic might offer more specialized care. On the other hand, pharmacies are not just for picking up prescriptions but often offer essential medical advice for minor ailments.

KEYWORDS/PHRASES AND HOW TO PRONOUNCE THEM:

1. *Fiebre* [fee•EH•bre] — (Fever)
2. *Tos* [TOHS] — (Cough)
3. *Dolor* [doh•LOR] — (Pain)
4. *Dolor de cabeza* [doh•LOR de kah•BEH•za] — (Headache)
5. *Estómago* [ehs•TOH•mah•go] — (Stomach)
6. *Hospital* [oh•pee•TAL] — (Hospital)
7. *Clínica* [KLEE•nee•kah] — (Clinic)
8. *Farmacia* [phar•mah•SEEA] — (Pharmacy)
9. *Medicina* [meh•dee•SEE•nah] — (Medicine)
10. *Receta* [reh•SEH•tah] — (Prescription)

Pharmacy Essentials

Pharmacies are pivotal in healthcare, especially when immediate attention is required for non-critical conditions. Learning how to request medications involves phrases like "*Necesito algo para...*" (I need something for...) followed by your symptom or condition. Understanding the pharmacist's questions, such as "*¿Es para usted?*" (Is it for you?) It helps provide the necessary details to receive the correct medication.

Over-the-counter (OTC) medications, "*medicamentos sin receta*," are widely available for common conditions. However, some medications that might be OTC in your home country could require a prescription, "*receta*," elsewhere. Thus, phrases like "*¿Necesito receta para esto?*" (Do I need a prescription for this?) become handy. Additionally, learning to read dosage instructions, *"instrucciones de dosis,"* ensures you use the medication safely.

KEYWORDS/PHRASES AND HOW TO PRONOUNCE THEM:

1. *Necesito algo para...* [neh•seh•SEE•toh AHL•goh PAH•rah] — (I need something for...)
2. *¿Es para usted?* [EHS PAH•rah oos•TED?] — (Is it for you?)
3. *Medicamentos sin receta* [meh•dee•ca•MEN•tos seen reh•SEH•tah] — (Over-the-counter (OTC) medications)
4. *Receta* [reh•SEH•tah] — (Prescription)
5. *Instrucciones de dosis* [eens•truk•see•OH•nes de DOH•sis] — (Dosage instructions)
6. *Dolor* [doh•LOR] — (Pain)
7. *Fiebre* [fee•EH•bre] — (Fever)
8. *Antibiótico* [an•tee•bee•OH•tee•koh] — (Antibiotic)
9. *Analgésico* [ah•nal•HEH•see•koh] — (Painkiller)
10. *Antihistamínico* [an•tee•ehs•tah•MEE•nee•koh] — (Antihistamine)
11. *Jarabe* [ha•RAH•beh] — (Syrup)

Handling Emergencies

In emergencies, quickly communicating the nature of an urgent situation is vital. Phrases like *"Necesito ayuda"* (I need help), *"Es una emergencia"* (It's an emergency), and *"Llame a una ambulancia*" (Call an ambulance) are critical. For identifying emergency services, familiarize yourself with terms such as "*servicios de emergencia*" (emergency services), "*bomberos*" (firefighters), and "*policía*" (police).

Clarifying the emergency can significantly impact the response time and assistance received. If someone is injured, stating "*Hay un herido*" (There is an injured person) followed by the specific issue, e.g., "*Está inconsciente*" (He/She is unconscious), effectively directs the emergency response. Knowing your location is equally important, so practicing how to describe your whereabouts is beneficial.

KEYWORDS/PHRASES AND HOW TO PRONOUNCE THEM:

1. *Necesito ayuda* [neh•se•SEE•to a•YOO•da] — (I need help)
2. *Es una emergencia* [es OO•na e•mer•HEN•see•a] — (It's an emergency)
3. *Llame a una ambulancia* [YAH•me a OO•na am•bu•LAN•see•a] — (Call an ambulance)
4. *Servicios de emergencia* [ser•VEE•see•os de e•mer•HEN•see•a] — (Emergency services)
5. *Bomberos* [bom•BEH•ros] — (Firefighters)
6. *Policía* [poh•lee•SEE•a] — (Police)
7. *Hay un herido* [eye oon eh•REE•do] — (There is an injured person)
8. *Está inconsciente* [ehs•TAH in•con•SYEN•te] — (He/She is unconscious)
9. *¿Dónde estamos?* [DON•de es•TAH•mos?] — (Where are we?)

10. *Necesitamos asistencia médica* [ne•se•see•TAH•mos
    as•sis•TEN•see•a MEH•dee•ka] — (We need
    medical assistance)

Cultural Considerations in Healthcare

Approaching healthcare in Hispanic countries with an understanding of cultural norms makes sure you have respectful and effective interactions. In many such countries, personal space and physical contact, like handshakes or a pat on the back are common and considered polite, even in professional settings like doctor's offices. However, maintaining formality in language, using "*usted*" instead of "*tú*," demonstrates respect, especially when speaking to medical professionals.

Appointments might adhere to something other than scheduled times, reflecting a more relaxed approach to time management. It is appreciated when people demonstrate patience and flexibility in these situations. While punctuality is valued, it's understood that delays can occur, especially in public healthcare facilities where resources might be stretched thin.

Privacy norms can also differ; don't be surprised if questions about your health are more direct or personal than what you're accustomed to. Answering these openly helps in accurate diagnosis and treatment. Additionally, it's common for family members to play an active role in patient care, both in decision-making and in providing support during appointments or hospital stays.

Navigating medical conversations and healthcare situations in Spanish-speaking environments takes a little bit more than language proficiency. It's about adapting to and respecting cultural practices, ensuring effective communication, and fostering meaningful interactions with healthcare providers. Equipping yourself with the necessary vocabulary and cultural understanding allows for a more comfortable and respectful experience, whether addressing a minor health issue at a pharmacy or navigating more serious medical emergencies.

KEYWORDS/PHRASES AND HOW TO PRONOUNCE THEM:

1. *Espacio personal* [ehs•PAH•see•oh per•soh•NAL] — (Personal space)
2. *Contacto físico* [con•TAK•toh FEE•see•koh] — (Physical contact)
3. *Usted; Tú* [oos•TED; TOO] — (You | "*usted*" for formal situations and "*tú*" for informal settings)
4. *Cita médica* [SEE•tah MEH•dee•kah] — (Medical appointment)
5. *Paciencia* [pah•SYEN•sya] — (Patience)
6. *Privacidad* [pree•vah•see•DAHD] — (Privacy)
7. *Preguntas directas* [preh•GOON•tas dee•REK•tas] — (Direct questions)
8. *Apoyo familiar* [ah•POH•yoh fah•mee•LEEAR] — (Family support)
9. *Toma de decisiones* [TOH•mah de deh•see•SEEOH•nes] - (Decision making)

10. *Flexibilidad* [flek•see•bee•lee•DAHD] — (Flexibility)

Chapter 1.6 Common Spanish Phrases

1. *Tengo fiebre y necesito algo para bajarla.* [TEN•go fee•EH•bre ee ne•se•SEE•to AHL•go PAH•ra bah•HAR•la.] — (I have a fever and need something to lower it.)

2. *¿Tiene algún analgésico para el dolor de cabeza?* [tee•EH•ne al•GOON a•nal•HEH•see•ko PAH•ra el do•LOR de ka•BEH•sa?] — (Do you have any painkillers for a headache?)

3. *Necesito una receta para este antibiótico.* [ne•se•SEE•to OO•na reh•SEH•ta PAH•ra EHS•te an•tee•bee•OH•tee•ko.] — (I need a prescription for this antibiotic.)

4. *¿Dónde está la farmacia más cercana?* [DON•deh es•TAH la far•MAH•see•a MAHS ser•KA•na?] — (Where is the nearest pharmacy?)

5. *Estoy en el hospital y necesito ayuda.* [es•TOI en el os•pee•TAL ee ne•se•SEE•to a•YOO•da.] — (I'm at the hospital and need help.)

6. *¿Es para usted este medicamento sin receta?* [ehs PAH•ra oos•TED EHS•te me•dee•ca•MEN•to sin re•SEH•ta?] — (Is this over-the-counter medication for you?)

7. *Tengo tos y dolor en el estómago.* [TEN•go tos ee do•LOR en el es•TOH•mah•go.] — (I have a cough and stomach pain.)

8. *Llame a una ambulancia, es una emergencia.*
   [YAH•me a OO•na am•bu•LAN•see•a, es OO•na
   e•mer•HEN•see•a.] — (Call an ambulance, it's an
   emergency.)

9. *¿Cuáles son las instrucciones de dosis para este jarabe?*
   [KWAH•les son las ins•truk•SYO•nes de DOH•sis
   PAH•ra EHS•te ha•RA•be?] — (What are the
   dosage instructions for this syrup?)

10. *Necesitamos asistencia médica para una persona
    herida.* [ne•se•see•TAH•mos a•sees•TEN•see•a
    MEH•dee•ka PAH•ra OO•na per•SO•na
    e•REE•da.] — (We need medical assistance for an
    injured person.)

Chapter 1.6 Worksheet:

Basic Health Vocabulary:

1) Fill in the blanks with the Spanish and English portions.

- Necesito algo para mi
  _____. (I need
  something for my
  _____.)
- Tengo mucha _____
  y me duele la garganta. (I have a lot
  of_____ and my
  throat hurts.)
- Mi _____ me duele
  mucho. (My _____
  hurts a lot.)

- Tengo fiebre y me siento muy
  _____. (I have a
  fever and I feel very
  _____.)
- Me duele la _____.
  (My _____ hurts.)

Pharmacy Essentials:

- ¿_____ receta para
  esto? (Do I need a prescription for this?)
- Necesito algo para la
  _____. (I need
  something for the
  _____.)
- ¿Tiene _____ para
  el dolor de cabeza? (Do you have
  _____ for
  headaches?)
- ¿Cuál es la _____
  de este medicamento? (What is the
  _____ of this
  medication?)
- ¿Dónde puedo encontrar
  _____? (Where can
  I find _____?)

Handling Emergencies:

- ¡_____ a una
  ambulancia! (Call an ambulance!)

- ¡_____ ayuda! (I need help!)
- Es una _____. (It's an emergency.)
- Hay un _____. (There is an injured person.)
- Necesito ir al

  _____. (I need to go to the _____.)

Cultural Considerations in Healthcare:

- Es importante mantener el

  _____ en los consultorios médicos." (It's important to maintain _____ in medical offices.)
- La _____ es valorada en las citas médicas. (Patience is valued in medical appointments.)
- La _____ de los pacientes debe ser respetada en todo momento. (The _____ of patients must be respected at all times.)
- La _____ es fundamental en la toma de decisiones médicas. (Family support is fundamental in medical decision-making.)
- Es esencial demostrar

  _____ al interactuar con los profesionales de la salud. (It's essential to show

_____ when

interacting with healthcare professionals.)

2) **Dialogue:** Doctor-Patient Conversation:

This is designed to enhance your Spanish language skills by focusing on practical dialogues between a doctor and a patient.

Pay close attention to the vocabulary, sentence structure and pronunciation tips throughout the conversation.

Doctor: *Buenos días, ¿cómo se siente hoy?*
[BWE•nos DEE•as, KOH•mo se SYEN•te O•y?]
(Good morning. How are you feeling today?)

Patient: *No me siento muy bien, doctor.*
[no meh SYEN•to MOO•ee bien, doc•TOR.]
(I don't feel very well, doctor.)

Doctor: *¿Qué síntomas tiene?*
[KEH SEEN•to•mas TYE•ne?]
(What symptoms do you have?)

Patient: Tengo fiebre y un dolor de cabeza constante.
[TEN•go FYE•bre ee oon do•LOR de ca•BEH•za cons•TAN•te.]
(I have a fever and a constant headache.)

Doctor: *Vamos a necesitar darle medicina para la fiebre y el dolor de cabeza.*
[VAH•mos a ne•ce•see•TAR DHAR•le me•dee•SEE•na PAH•ra la FYE•bre ee el do•LOR de ca•BEH•za.]
(We will need to give you medicine for the fever and the headache.)

Patient: *¿Necesito una receta para esos medicamentos?*
[ne•ce•SEE•to OO•na re•SE•ta PAH•ra esos me•di•ca•MEN•tos?]
(Do I need a prescription for those medications?)

Doctor: *Sí, le escribiré una receta para un antibiótico y un analgésico. Es importante que siga las instrucciones de dosis exactamente como están escritas.*
[SEE, le es•kree•bee•REH OO•na re•SE•ta PAH•ra oon an•tee•bee•OH•tee•koh ee oon ah•nal•HEH•see•koh. ehs eem•por•TAN•teh keh SEE•gah lahs ins•truk•SYO•nes de DO•sis ehks•sak•tah•MEN•teh KOH•moh ehs•TAN ehs•KREE•tas.]
(Yes, I will write you a prescription for an antibiotic and a painkiller. It is important that you follow the dosage instructions exactly as they are written.)

Patient: *¿Y si tengo efectos secundarios?*
[ee see TEN•go e•FEK•tos se•cun•DAH•rios?]
(What if I have side effects?)

Doctor: Si experimenta cualquier efecto secundario, debe venir a la clínica inmediatamente. Quisiera verlo de nuevo en una semana para seguimiento.

[see eks•peh•ree•MEN•tah KWAL•kyer eh•FEK•toh
se•koon•DAH•reeo, DEH•be ve•NEER a la KLEE•nee•kah
een•meh•dya•tah•MEN•teh. kee•SYE•rah VER•loh en
OO•na se•MAH•na PAH•ra se•gee•MYEN•toh.]
(If you experience any side effects, you should come to the
clinic immediately. I would like to see you for a follow-up in
a week.)

Patient: *Gracias, doctor. Seguiré las instrucciones cuida-
dosamente.*
[GRA•seeas, doc•TOR. se•gee•REH las ins•truk•SYO•nes
cui•da•DO•sa•men•te.]
(Thank you, doctor. I will follow the instructions carefully.)

1.7 Accommodation and Reservations: Booking Your Stay

Deciding where to stay is as thrilling as it is crucial when
planning a trip to a new place. Your chosen place becomes
your temporary home, a base from which all your adventures begin and end. Here, we'll cover how to navigate the
world of accommodations, ensuring your stay is comfortable
and enriches your travel experience.

Types of Accommodation

The Spanish language offers a rich vocabulary to describe
various types of lodging, catering to every traveler's preferences and budget. "*Hoteles*" (hotels) range from the luxurious
"*hotel de cinco estrellas*" (five-star hotel) to the more budget-
friendly "*hotel de dos estrellas*" (two-star hotel), providing
options for different levels of comfort and amenities. For

those seeking a more communal or economical stay, *"hostales"* (hostels) present a vibrant, shared environment, often with *"dormitorios"* (dormitory rooms) where travelers can meet and share stories.

"Alquileres vacacionales" (vacation rentals) like *"apartamentos"* (apartments) offer travelers a home away from home, complete with kitchens and living spaces, ideal for more extended stays or groups. Meanwhile, *"casas rurales"* (country houses) immerse guests in the countryside's tranquility, offering a slice of local life away from the urban hustle.

Choosing the right type involves weighing cost against comfort and considering what experiences you wish to gain. Each option provides a unique window into the local culture, from the communal tables of a hostel to the privacy of a rented apartment in a bustling neighborhood.

KEYWORDS/PHRASES AND HOW TO PRONOUNCE THEM:

1. Hoteles [o•TEH•les] — (Hotels)

- *"Busco un hotel"* — (I'm looking for a hotel.)

2. Hotel de cinco estrellas [o•TEL de SEEN•koh es•TRE•yas] — (Five-star hotel)

- *"Prefiero un hotel de cinco estrellas por las comodidades de lujo."* — (I prefer a five-star hotel for luxury amenities.)

3. Hotel de dos estrellas [o•TEL de dos es•TRE•yas] — (Two-star hotel)

- *"Necesitamos un hotel de dos estrellas económico."* — (We need a budget-friendly, two-star hotel.)

4. Hostales [ohs•TAH•les] — (Hostels)

- *"¿Hay hostales baratos cerca?"* — (Are there any cheap hostels nearby?)

5. Dormitorios [dor•mee•TOH•ree•ohs] — (Dormitory rooms)

- *"Los hostales suelen tener dormitorios."* — (Hostels usually have dormitory rooms.)

6. Alquileres vacacionales [al•kee•LEH•res va•kah•SEEOH•nah•les] — (Vacation rentals) /al-ki-le-res va-ca-cio-na-les/

- *"Me interesan los alquileres vacacionales para nuestra estancia."* — (I'm interested in vacation rentals for our stay.)

7. Apartamentos [ah•par•tah•MEN•tos] — (Apartments)

- *"¿Tienen apartamentos disponibles?"* — (Do you have apartments available?)

8. *Casas rurales* [KAH•sas roo•RAH•les] — (Country houses)

- *"Nos encantaría experimentar la estancia en una casa rural."* — (We'd love to experience staying in a country house.)

9. *Económico* [eh•koh•NOH•mee•koh] — (Budget-friendly)

- *"Buscamos un alojamiento económico."* — (We're looking for a budget-friendly accommodation.)

10. *Lujo* [LOO•ho] — (Luxury)

- *"Ofrecen comodidades de lujo."* — (They offer luxury amenities.)

Making Reservations

Once you've selected your preferred accommodation, securing your stay is next. Modern conveniences allow various booking methods, from online platforms to direct calls. However, understanding key phrases can smooth this process considerably. *"Quisiera reservar..."* (I would like to book...) is a straightforward start, followed by your specifics, such as *"una habitación individual"* (a single room) for one or *"una habitación doble"* (a double room) for two.

Inquiring about amenities can significantly enhance your stay. Questions like *"¿Incluye desayuno la habitación?"* (Does the room include breakfast?) or *"¿Tiene acceso a WiFi?"* (Is there WiFi access?) Ensure your needs are met. For those with particular preferences, specifying *"una habitación con vista al mar"* (a room with a sea view) or *"un apartamento con cocina"* (an apartment with a kitchen) tailors your accommodation to your desires.

Remember, booking in advance, *"reservar con antelación,"* secures your spot and often unlocks better rates and choices. Confirming your reservation, *"confirmar la reserva,"* through a follow-up email or call ensures no surprises upon arrival.

KEYWORDS/PHRASES AND HOW TO PRONOUNCE THEM:

1. *Quisiera reservar...* [kee•SYE•ra reh•ser•VAR] — (I would like to book...)
2. *"Quisiera reservar una habitación individual."* — (I would like to book a single room.)
3. *Una habitación individual...* [OO•na a•bee•ta•see•ON in•dee•vee•doo•AHL] — (A single room)
4. *"Necesito una habitación individual para mi estancia."* — (I need a single room for my stay.)
5. *Una habitación doble* [OO•na a•bee•ta•see•ON DOH•ble] — (A double room)
6. *"Nos gustaría reservar una habitación doble."* — (We'd like to book a double room.)
7. *¿Incluye desayuno la habitación?* [een•KLOO•ye deh•sa•YOO•no la a•bee•ta•see•ON?] — (Does the room include breakfast?)
8. *"Me pregunto si la habitación incluye desayuno."* — (I'm wondering if the room includes breakfast.)

9. *¿Tiene acceso a WiFi?* [tee•eh•ne ak•se•so a WiFi?] — (Is there WiFi access?)

10. *"¿Tiene nuestra habitación acceso a WiFi?"* — (Does our room have WiFi access?)

11. *Una habitación con vista al mar* [OO•na a•bee•ta•see•ON kon VEES•ta al mar] — (A room with a sea view)

12. *"Prefiero una habitación con vista al mar."* — (I prefer a room with a sea view.)

13. *Un apartamento con cocina* [oon a•par•ta•MEN•to kon ko•SEE•na] — (An apartment with a kitchen)

14. *"Necesitamos un apartamento con cocina."* — (We need an apartment with a kitchen.)

15. *Reservar con antelación* [re•ser•VAR kon an•te•la•see•ON] — (Book in advance)

16. *"Es mejor reservar con antelación."* — (It's better to book in advance.)

17. *Confirmar la reserva* [kon•feer•MAR la re•SER•va] — (Confirm the reservation)

18. *"Por favor, confirmar la reserva."* — (Please confirm the reservation.)

19. *¿Cuál es el precio por noche?* [KWAL es el PRE•see•o por NOH•che?] — (What is the price per night?)

20. *"Me gustaría saber ¿Cuál es el precio por noche?"* — (I'd like to know the price per night.)

Checking In and Out

Arriving at your accommodation marks the beginning of your stay, and a smooth check-in sets the tone. Presenting yourself, *"Me llamo..."* (My name is...), followed by *"tengo una reserva"* (I have a reservation), initiates the process. It's here, you might ask, *"¿A qué hora es el check-out?"* (What time is check-out?), clarifying departure details early to plan your last day without rush.

Requests at this stage, such as asking for a *"mapa de la ciudad"* (city map) or recommendations for *"restaurantes cercanos"* (nearby restaurants), not only aid in your exploration but also engage with the staff, often leading to insightful local tips.

On the other hand, checking out usually requires a simple *"Quisiera hacer el check-out"* (I would like to check out). This is the time to settle any *"cargos adicionales"* (additional charges) you may have incurred and return keys or cards. Expressing gratitude, *"Gracias por su hospitalidad"* (Thank you for your hospitality), leaves a lasting positive impression, acknowledging the role of your hosts in your travel experience.

KEYWORDS/PHRASES AND HOW TO PRONOUNCE THEM:

1. *Me llamo...* [meh YAH•moh] — (My name is...)
2. Upon arrival, introduce yourself with *"Me llamo...".*
3. *Tengo una reserva* [TEHN•goh OO•nah reh•SER•vah] — (I have a reservation)
4. Start the check-in process by stating *"Tengo una reserva."*
5. *¿A qué hora es el check-out?* [ah KEH O•rah ehs el check-out] — (What time is check-out?)
6. To plan your departure, ask *"¿A qué hora es el check-out?."*

7. *Mapa de la ciudad* [MAH•pah deh lah
   see•oo•DAHD] — (City map)

8. Requesting a *"mapa de la ciudad"* can help you
   navigate the area.

9. *Restaurantes cercanos* [rehs•tah•oo•RAN•tes
   ser•KAH•nos] — (Nearby restaurants)

10. For local dining options, ask about *"restaurantes
    cercanos."*

11. *Quisiera hacer el check-out* [kee•see•EH•rah
    ah•SER el check-out] — (I would like to
    check out)

12. When leaving, say *"Quisiera hacer el check-out"* to
    initiate the process.

13. *Cargos adicionales* [KAR•gos
    ah•dee•see•oh•NAH•les] — (Additional charges)

14. Inquire about any "cargos adicionales" before
    finalizing your bill.

15. *Gracias por su hospitalidad* [GRAH•seeas por soo
    ohs•pee•tah•lee•DAHD] — (Thank you for your
    hospitality)

16. Expressing gratitude with "Gracias por su
    hospitalidad" is a courteous way to end your stay.

17. *¿Puedo dejar mi equipaje aquí?* [poo•EH•doh
    deh•HAR mee eh•kee•PAH•heh ah•KEE] — (Can
    I leave my luggage here?)

18. If you need to store your luggage, ask "¿Puedo dejar
    mi equipaje aquí?."

19. *¿Cuál es el código WiFi?* [KWAL ehs ehl KOH•dee•go
    WiFi] — (What is the WiFi code?)

20. Stay connected by asking "¿Cuál es el código WiFi?"
    upon arrival.

Problem-Solving at Your Accommodation

Even with the best planning, issues can arise. Perhaps the room doesn't meet your expectations, "*la habitación no coincide con la descripción*" (the room doesn't match the description), or there's a need for "*toallas adicionales*" (additional towels). Addressing these concerns politely and directly, "*Disculpe, ¿podría resolver un problema con mi habitación?*" (Excuse me, could you solve a problem with my room?), encourages swift resolution.

In more significant situations, like a "*fuga de agua*" (water leak) or "*el aire acondicionado no funciona*" (the air conditioning isn't working), knowing how to describe the issue ensures that your comfort is quickly restored. Patience and understanding go a long way, especially when navigating unexpected challenges in a new language.

For requests beyond the basics, such as "*¿Es posible cambiar de habitación?*" (Is it possible to change rooms?) or "*Necesito hacer el check-out más tarde*" (I need to check out later), being transparent and polite in your communication respects the staff's ability to accommodate your needs within their means.

In essence, navigating accommodation and reservations in Spanish-speaking destinations is more than a transaction; it's an exchange that offers glimpses into local hospitality, practices, and, occasionally, challenges. Armed with the correct vocabulary and a respectful approach, each interaction becomes an opportunity to deepen your connection to the language and the people who speak it, turning every stay into a memorable part of your adventure.

KEYWORDS/PHRASES AND HOW TO PRONOUNCE THEM:

1. *La habitación no coincide con la descripción* [lah a•bee•ta•see•ON no koh•een•SEE•deh kon lah dehs•kreep•see•ON] — (The room doesn't match the description)

2. *Toallas adicionales* [toh•AH•yas ah•dee•see•oh•NAH•les] — (Additional towels)

3. *Disculpe, ¿podría resolver un problema con mi habitación?* [dees•KOOL•peh, poh•DREE•ah reh•sohl•VEHR oon proh•BLEH•mah kon mee ah•bee•tah•SYOHN?] — (Excuse me, could you solve a problem with my room?)

4. *Fuga de agua* [FOO•gah deh AH•gwah] — (Water leak)

5. *El aire acondicionado no funciona* [el AH•ee•reh ah•kohn•dee•see•oh•NAH•doh noh foon•see•OH•nah] — (The air conditioning isn't working)

6. *¿Es posible cambiar de habitación?* [ehs poh•SEE•bleh kahm•bee•ahr deh ah•bee•tah•SYOHN?] — (Is it possible to change rooms?)

7. *Necesito hacer el check-out más tarde* [neh•seh•SEE•toh ah•SEHR el check-out MAHS TAR•deh] — (I need to check out later)

8. *¿Podría tener un adaptador?* [poh•DREE•ah teh•NEHR oon ah•dap•tah•DOR?] — (Could I have an adapter?)

9. *El WiFi no funciona* [ehl WiFi noh
foon•see•OH•nah] — (The WiFi isn't working)

10. *¿Puede enviarme a alguien para arreglarlo?*
[PWEH•deh en•vee•AHR•meh ah AHL•gyen
PAH•rah ah•rrehGLAR•loh?] — (Can you send
someone to fix it?)

Chapter 1.7 Common Spanish Phrases

1. *¿Cuánto cuesta una noche en un hotel de cinco estrellas?*
[KWAN•toh KWES•tah OO•nah NOH•cheh en
oon o•TEL de SEEN•ko es•TRE•yas?] — (How
much does one night in a five-star hotel cost?)

2. *En los hostales, ¿puedo encontrar habitaciones
privadas?* [ehn los os•TAH•les, PWEH•doh
en•kon•TRAR ah•bee•tah•see•OH•nes
pree•VAH•das?] — (In hostels, can I find private
rooms?)

3. *Preferimos alquileres vacacionales para sentirnos como
en casa.* [preh•feh•REE•mos al•ki•LEH•res
va•ca•cio•NAH•les PAH•ra sen•TEER•nos
KOH•mo en KAH•sah.] — (We prefer vacation
rentals to feel at home.)

4. *Buscamos una casa rural con encanto para el fin de
semana.* [boos•KAH•mos OO•nah KAH•sa
roo•RAL kon en•KAHN•toh PAH•ra el feen de
se•MAH•nah.] — (We are looking for a charming
country house for the weekend.)

5. *¿Ofrecen servicios de lujo en este apartamento?*
[o•FREH•sen ser•VEE•see•os de LOO•ho en

EHS•teh a•par•ta•MEN•to?] — (Do they offer
luxury services in this apartment?)

6. *Quisiera un dormitorio con baño privado.*
[key•see•EH•rah oon dor•mi•TOH•rio kon
BAHN•yo pree•VAH•do.] — (I would like a
bedroom with a private bathroom.)

7. *¿Este hotel de dos estrellas tiene desayuno incluido?*
[EHS•te o•TEL de dos es•TRE•yas TYEH•ne
deh•sa•YOO•no een•kloo•EE•do?] — (Does this
two-star hotel include breakfast?)

8. *Me gustaría un alojamiento económico pero cómodo.*
[meh goos•tah•REE•ah oon a•lo•ha•mee•EN•to
e•co•NOH•mi•co PEH•ro KOH•mo•do.] — (I
would like a budget-friendly but comfortable
accommodation.)

9. *¿Hay WiFi gratuito en los dormitorios de este hostal?*
[eye WiFi grah•too•EE•to en los dor•mi•TOH•rios
de EHS•te os•TAL?] — (Is there free WiFi in the
dormitories of this hostel?)

10. *Para una experiencia única, prefiero una casa rural
sobre un apartamento.* [PAH•ra OO•nah
eks•peh•ree•EHN•see•ah OO•nee•ka,
preh•fee•EH•ro OO•nah KAH•sah roo•RAL
SOH•bre oon a•par•ta•MEN•to.] — (For a unique
experience, I prefer a country house over an
apartment.)

Chapter 1.7 Worksheet

Types of Accommodations

1) Fill in the blanks with the correct Spanish words.

- A place offering temporary lodging for travelers (*hotel*):

  _____

- A rented property where tourists can stay, usually with more space than a hotel room (*apartment*):

  _____

- A budget-friendly accommodation offering shared rooms (*hostel*):

  _____

- Luxurious accommodation offering various amenities (*resort*):

  _____

Making Reservations

- Tengo una (reservation):

  _____

- Me llamo [your name]:

  _____

- ¿Tiene (rooms)

  _____ disponibles?

Checking In and Out

- ¿A qué hora es el (check-out)?:

  _____

- Quisiera hacer el (check-out):

  _____

- ¿Puedo dejar mi (luggage) aquí?:

  _____

Problem-Solving at Your Accommodation

- La habitación no (coincides) con la descripción:

  _____

- Disculpe, ¿podría (solve) un problema con mi
  habitación?:

  _____

- El aire acondicionado no (is working):

  _____

- Necesito hacer el check-out (later):

  _____

2) **Dialogue:** Conversation between a Guest and the Receptionist at a Hotel.

Guest: _Hola, quisiera reservar una habitación doble para el próximo fin de semana._
[O•lah, kee•SYEH•rah reh•sehr•VAHR OO•nah ah•bee•tah•SYOHN DOH•bleh pah•rah el PROKS•ee•moh feen deh seh•MAH•nah.]
(Hello, I would like to book a double room for next weekend.)

Receptionist: _Claro, ¿incluye desayuno la reserva?_
[KLAH•roh, een•KLOO•yeh deh•sah•YOO•noh lah reh•SEHR•vah?]
(Of course, does the reservation include breakfast?)

Guest: _Sí, y ¿tiene acceso a WiFi?_
[SEE, ee TYEH•neh ahk•SEH•soh ah WiFi?]
(Yes, and is there WiFi access?)

Receptionist: _Sí, todas nuestras habitaciones tienen WiFi. ¿A nombre de quién hago la reserva?_
[SEE, TOH•dahs NWES•trahs ah•bee•tah•SYOH•nes

TYEH•nen WiFi. ah NOHM•breh deh KYEHN AH•goh lah
reh•SEHR•vah?]
(Yes, all our rooms have WiFi. Under whose name should I
make the reservation?)

Guest: *A nombre de Juan Pérez.*
[ah NOHM•breh deh HWAN PEH•rehz.]
(Under the name Juan Pérez.)

Receptionist: *Perfecto, Juan. Su reserva está confirmada. ¿A qué
hora planea hacer el check-in?*
[Per•FEK•toh, HWAN. soo reh•SEHR•vah ehs•TAH
kon•feer•MAH•dah. Ah KEH O•rah plah•NEH•ah
ah•SER el check-in?]
(Perfect, Juan. Your reservation is confirmed. What time do
you plan to check in?)

Guest: *Llegaré alrededor de las tres de la tarde.*
[yeh•gah•REH ahl•reh•deh•DOR deh lahs tres deh lah
TAR•deh.]
(I will arrive around three in the afternoon.)

Receptionist: *Excelente. Nos vemos entonces.*
[eks•seh•LEN•teh. nohs VEH•mos en•TON•ses.]
(Excellent. See you then.)

1.8 Work and Professions: Talking About Your Job

When you find yourself in the company of new acquain-
tances or networking in a Spanish-speaking environment,
the conversation often steers toward professions and work-

places. In these moments, your ability to describe what you do, where you work, and your professional aspirations in Spanish can bridge cultural and linguistic gaps, fostering meaningful and beneficial connections.

Describing Your Profession

Starting with the basics, "*Soy...*" followed by your profession, such as "*Soy ingeniero*" (I'm an engineer) or "*Soy maestra*" (I'm a teacher), sets the stage. Expanding on this by mentioning your specialization or industry, for example, "*en tecnología de la información*" (in information technology) or "*en educación primaria*" (in primary education), paints a more detailed picture of your professional landscape.

Discussing your responsibilities offers insights into your daily work life. Phrases like "*Me encargo de...*" (I'm in charge of...) or "*Mi trabajo consiste en...*" (My job consists of...) followed by your tasks, such as "*gestionar proyectos*" (manage projects) or "*desarrollar planes de estudio*" (develop curriculums), highlighting your role and contributions. This shares aspects of your professional identity and opens avenues for a deeper conversation about shared interests or expertise.

KEYWORDS/PHRASES AND HOW TO PRONOUNCE THEM:

1. Soy... [SOI] — (I am...)

- *Soy ingeniero* [SOI een•heh•NYE•ro] — (I'm an engineer)
- *Soy maestra* [SOI mah•EHS•tra] — (I'm a teacher)

2. *En tecnología de la información* [ehn tek•no•loh•HEE•ah de lah een•for•mah•see•ON] — (In information technology)

3. *En educación primaria* [ehn eh•doo•kah•see•ON pree•MAH•ree•ah] — (In primary education)

4. *Me encargo de...* [meh ehn•KAR•go deh...] — (I'm in charge of...)

- *Gestionar proyectos* [hes•tyo•NAR pro•YEK•tos] — (Manage projects)
- *Desarrollar planes de estudio* [deh•sah•rro•YAR deh ehs•TOO•dyo] — (Develop curriculums)

5. *Mi trabajo consiste en...* [mee trah•BAH•hoh con•SEES•teh ehn...] — (My job consists of...)

- Followed by tasks like *gestionar proyectos* or *desarrollar planes de estudio.*

6. *Ingeniero* [een•heh•NYE•roh] — (Engineer)

7. *Maestra* [mah•EHS•tra] — (Teacher)

8. *Tecnología de la información* [tek•noh•loh•GEE•ah de lah een•for•mah•see•ON] — (Information technology)

9. *Educación primaria* [eh•doo•kah•see•ON pree•MAH•ree•ah] — (Primary education)

10. *Gestionar* [hes•tyo•NAR] — (Manage)

11. *Desarrollar* [deh•sah•rro•YAR] — (Develop)

Workplace Vocabulary

"*La oficina*" (the office) or "*el lugar de trabajo*" (workplace,) has vocabularies that enrich conversations and make discussions about your professional environment more engaging. Key terms include "*compañeros de trabajo*" (coworkers), "*jefe*" (boss), and "*departamento*" (department), which help you describe the people and structures that define your work setting.

Meetings, "*reuniones*," are a staple of professional life. They come with phrases like "*organizar reuniones*" (organize meetings) or "*asistir a conferencias*" (attend conferences), offering glimpses into your collaborative and learning activities at work. Discussing projects, "*proyectos*," and deadlines, "*fechas límite*," further delves into the dynamics and pressures of your job, resonating with those familiar with the hustle of meeting targets and achieving goals.

KEYWORDS/PHRASES AND HOW TO PRONOUNCE THEM:

1. *La oficina* [lah oh•fee•SEE•nah] — (The office)
2. *El lugar de trabajo* [ehl loo•GAHR deh trah•BAH•ho] — (The workplace)
3. *Compañeros de trabajo* [kohm•pah•NYE•ros deh tra•BAH•ho] — (Coworkers)
4. *Jefe* [HEH•feh] — (Boss)
5. *Departamento* [deh•par•ta•MEN•toh] — (Department)
6. *Reuniones* [reh•oo•NYO•nes] — (Meetings)

7. *Organizar reuniones* [ohr•gah•nee•SAHR reh•oo•NYO•nes] — (Organize meetings)
8. *Asistir a conferencias* [ah•sees•TEER ah kohn•feh•REN•syas] — (Attend conferences)
9. *Proyectos* [pro•YEK•tos] — (Projects)
10. *Fechas límite* [FEH•chas LEE•mee•teh] — (Deadlines)
11. *Organizar* [or•gah•nee•SAHR] — (Organize)
12. *Asistir* [ah•ten•DEHR] — (Attend)

Job Hunting Language

Knowing how to navigate job hunting in Spanish can be invaluable for those venturing into the job market. Starting with *"buscar trabajo"* (looking for a job) to *"enviar un currículum"* (sending a resume), these phrases are your initial steps toward securing opportunities. In interviews, *"entrevistas,"* expressing your skills, *"habilidades,"* and experiences, *"experiencias,"* convincingly can make a significant difference. Phrases like *"Tengo experiencia en..."* (I have experience in...) or *"Mis habilidades incluyen..."* (My skills include...) Set the foundation for a compelling narrative about your professional journey.

Questions commonly asked in interviews, such as *"¿Por qué quieres trabajar con nosotros?"* (Why do you want to work with us?) or *"¿Cuáles son tus objetivos profesionales?"* (What are your professional goals?), require thoughtful preparation. Answering these in fluent Spanish and with genuine insights into your aspirations and how they align with the potential employer's vision demonstrates both your linguistic proficiency and competence as well as commitment to your career path.

KEYWORDS/PHRASES AND HOW TO PRONOUNCE THEM:

1. *Buscar trabajo* [boo•KAR trah•BAH•ho] — (Looking for a job)
2. *Enviar un currículum* [en•vee•AR un koo•RREE•ku•lum] — (Sending a resume)
3. *Entrevistas* [en•treh•VEES•tas] — (Interviews)
4. *Habilidades* [ah•bee•lee•DAH•des] — (Skills)
5. *Experiencias* [eks•peh•ree•EN•see•as] — (Experiences)
6. *Tengo experiencia en...* [TEN•goh eks•peh•ree•EN•seea en...] — (I have experience in...)
7. *Mis habilidades incluyen...* [mees ah•bee•lee•DAH•des een•KLOO•yen...] — (My skills include...)
8. *¿Por qué quieres trabajar con nosotros?* [por KHE kee•EH•res trah•bah•HAR kon no•SO•tros] — (Why do you want to work with us?)
9. *¿Cuáles son tus objetivos profesionales?* [KWA•les son toos ob•heh•TEE•vos pro•feh•syo•NAH•les] — (What are your professional goals?)
10. *Experiencia laboral* [eks•peh•ree•EN•seeah lah•boh•RAL] — (Work experience)

Cultural Insights into Work Life

Understanding work culture in Spanish-speaking countries provides context to your conversations about professions and workplaces. For starters, *"horario de trabajo,"* work hours often extend beyond the typical 9-to-5, with a longer midday break, *"descanso del mediodía,"* in many regions. This break, a time for lunch and rest, underscores a balanced approach to work and leisure, a concept that might be novel to those from cultures with continuous workdays.

The concept of *"sobremesa,"* the time spent at the table talking after a meal, extends into professional settings, fostering relationships beyond mere work transactions. It illustrates the value of personal connections and their role in professional interactions and decision-making processes.

Networking, *"hacer contactos,"* is both formal and informal, with a significant emphasis on building trust, *"confianza,"* and rapport. Events and gatherings, professionally oriented or otherwise, serve as venues for expanding your professional circle, where a friendly demeanor and genuine interest in others pave the way for future collaborations.

Lastly, titles and formality hold weight in professional settings. Addressing colleagues and superiors with appropriate titles and a respectful tone, *"usted"* instead of *"tú,"* in initial meetings is customary, reflecting deference and professionalism. Observing these nuances not only aids in smooth communication but also demonstrates your respect for local customs and practices.

Navigating conversations about work and professions in Spanish-speaking environments is an enriching experience that extends far beyond mere language proficiency. It's an opportunity to share and learn about diverse professional landscapes, to connect over shared challenges and triumphs, and to weave your professional narrative into the rich tapestry of the global workplace. Whether describing your job, discussing workplace dynamics, exploring new opportunities, or delving into cultural nuances, each conversation is a step toward greater understanding and connection in the professional world.

KEYWORDS/PHRASES AND HOW TO PRONOUNCE THEM:

1. *Horario de trabajo* [oh•RAH•ree•oh deh trah•BAH•ho] — (Work hours)
2. *Descanso del mediodía* [des•KAHN•so del meh•dee•oh•DEE•ah] — (Midday break)
3. *Sobremesa* [soh•breh•MEH•sah] — (Time spent talking after a meal)
4. *Hacer contactos* [ah•SEHR kon•TAHK•tos] — (Networking)
5. *Confianza* [kon•fee•AHN•zah] — (Trust)
6. *Rapport* [rah•POR] — (Rapport | Pronounced similarly to the English word)
7. *Usted* [oos•TED] — (You, formal)
8. *Tú* [TOO] — (You, informal)
9. *Títulos* [TEE•too•lohs] — (Titles)
10. *Respeto* [res•PEH•to] — (Respect)

Chapter 1.8 Common Spanish Phrases

1. *Soy ingeniero en tecnología de la información.* [SOI een•heh•NYE•roh en tek•no•lo•HEE•ah de lah een•for•mah•see•ON] — (I am an engineer in information technology.)

2. *Me encargo de gestionar proyectos en mi oficina.* [me en•KAR•go de hes•tyo•NAR pro•YEK•tos en mi oh•fee•SEE•nah] — (I'm in charge of managing projects in my office.)

3. *Mi trabajo consiste en desarrollar planes de estudio para educación primaria.* [mee tra•BAH•ho kon•SEES•teh deh•sah•rro•YAR PLA•nes deh ehs•TOO•dyo PAH•ra eh•doo•ka•SYON pree•MAH•ree•ah] — (My job consists of developing curriculums for primary education.)

4. *Tengo experiencia en organizar reuniones con compañeros de trabajo.* [TEN•goh eks•peh•ree•EN•see•ah en or•gah•nee•SAR reh•oo•NYO•nes con kohm•pah•NYE•ros de tra•BAH•ho] — (I have experience in organizing meetings with coworkers.)

5. *Busco trabajo como maestra en educación primaria.* [boos•KAR tra•BAH•ho KOH•mo ma•EHS•tra en eh•doo•kah•SYON pree•MAH•ree•ah] — (I'm looking for a job as a teacher in primary education.)

6. *Mis habilidades incluyen hablar en público y asistir a conferencias.* [mees ah•bee•lee•DAH•des in•KLOO•yen ah•BLAR en POO•blee•ko ee ah•sees•TEER a kohn•feh•REN•see•as] — (My

skills include public speaking and attending conferences.)

7. *¿Cuáles son tus objetivos profesionales en el lugar de trabajo?* [KWAH•les son toos ohb•heh•TEE•vos pro•feh•syoh•NAH•les en el loo•GAR de tra•BAH•ho?] — (What are your professional goals at the workplace?)

8. *Envío mi currículum para aplicar al departamento de tecnología de la información.* [en•VEE•oh mee koo•RREE•ku•lum PAH•ra ah•plee•KAR al deh•par•tah•MEN•to de tek•noh•loh•HEE•ah de la een•for•mah•SYON] — (I am sending my resume to apply to the information technology department.)

9. *Después del almuerzo, disfrutamos de la sobremesa hablando sobre proyectos futuros.* [des•PWES del ahl•MWER•zo, dis•froo•TAH•mos de la soh•bre•MEH•sa ha•BLAN•do SOH•bre pro•YEK•tos foo•TOO•ros] — (After lunch, we enjoy the time spent talking about future projects.)

10. *¿Por qué quieres trabajar con nosotros como ingeniero?* [por KEH kee•EH•res tra•ba•HAR kon no•SO•tros KOH•mo in•he•NYE•ro?] — (Why do you want to work with us as an engineer?)

Chapter 1.8 Worksheet

Describing Your Profession

1) Fill in the blanks with the correct Spanish portions.

- Soy _____ (*I'm an engineer/teacher | or whatever your work is*).
- Trabajo en _____ (*in information technology/primary education*).
- Me encargo de
_____ (*I'm in charge of managing projects/developing curriculums*).

Workplace Vocabulary

- Mis compañeros de trabajo
_____ (*my coworkers*).
- Mi jefe _____ (*my boss*).
- Trabajo en el departamento de
_____ (*the department*).

Job Hunting Language

- Estoy buscando trabajo en
_____ (*looking for a job*).
- Envié mi currículum a

_____ (*sending a resume*).

- Tengo experiencia en

  _____ (*I have experience in...*).

Cultural Insights into Work Life

- El horario de trabajo en este país incluye

  _____ (*work hours*).
- El descanso del mediodía es para

  _____ (*midday break*).
- Después de comer, participamos en la sobremesa, que es _____

  (*time spent talking after a meal*).

2) **Dialogue:** Focus on the essential greetings, workplace vocabulary, and cultural nuances, emphasizing the importance of pronunciation and polite requests for navigating professional settings.

Co-worker 1: *Hola, soy nuevo. Soy ingeniero.*
[O•lah, soi NWE•voh. soi een•heh•NYE•roh.]
(Hello, I'm new. I'm an engineer.)

Co-worker 2: ¡Hola! Soy Marta, trabajo en marketing.
[O•lah! soi MAR•tah, trah•BAH•ho en MAR•keh•ting.]
Translation: Hello! I'm Marta, I work in marketing.

Co-worker 1: *Mucho gusto, Marta. ¿Puedes ayudarme con el horario?*
[MOO•choh GOOS•toh, Marta. PWE•des ah•yoo•DAR•meh con el oh•RAH•ree•oh?]
(Nice to meet you, Marta. Can you help me with the schedule?)

Co-worker 2: *Claro, el horario es flexible. A veces, charlamos después de comer.*
[KLAH•ro, el oh•RAH•ree•oh es flehk•SEE•bleh. ah VEH•sez, char•LAH•mos des•PWES deh koh•MER.]
(Sure, the schedule is flexible. Sometimes, we chat after eating.)

Co-worker 1: *Qué bien. ¿Cómo es trabajar aquí?*
[KEH byen. KOH•moh es trah•bah•HAR ah•KEE?]
(That's good. What is it like to work here?)

Co-worker 2: *Es colaborativo. Nos gusta la confianza y conocer gente.*
[ehs koh•lah•boh•rah•TEE•voh. nos GOOS•tah la kon•FYAN•sah ee koh•no•SER HEN•teh.]
(It's collaborative. We like trust and meeting people.)

Co-worker 1: *Genial. Quiero aportar con lo que sé.*
[heh•nee•AHL. KYEH•ro ah•por•TAR con lo keh SEH.]
(Great. I want to contribute with what I know.)

Co-worker 2: *Seguro. Aquí valoramos a todos. Bienvenido.*
[seh•GOO•ro. ah•KEE vah•loh•RAH•mos ah TOH•dos. byen•veh•NEE•doh.]

(Of course. Here, we value everyone. Welcome.)

1.9 Leisure and Entertainment: Discussing Interests and Planning Outings

In the vibrant tapestry of Spanish-speaking societies, leisure and entertainment form the colorful threads that bind communities, spark friendships, and ignite passions. Whether you're an aficionado of the arts or a devotee of the great outdoors, sharing your interests and planning social activities in Spanish enriches your experience and connects you more profoundly with the culture and its people.

Talking about Hobbies

Engaging in conversations about hobbies invites a peek into each other's worlds, revealing shared interests or introducing new passions. When you express your hobbies, like *"Me gusta la fotografía"* (I like photography) or *"Soy aficionado/a del fútbol"* (I'm a soccer fan), you're not just sharing an activity; you're opening the door to your world. This exchange often leads to stories, tips, and plans to enjoy these activities together.

For those keen on learning from these interactions, questions such as *"¿Qué te gusta hacer en tu tiempo libre?"* (What do you like to do in your free time?) or *"¿Tienes algún hobby?"* (Do you have any hobbies?) serve as bridges to understanding personal interests and cultural nuances. Perhaps you'll discover a local passion for *"jugar al padel,"* a racket sport that's wildly popular in certain Spanish-speaking countries, sparking a new interest or even a friendly match.

KEYWORDS/PHRASES AND HOW TO PRONOUNCE THEM:

1. *Hobbies/Aficiones* [ah•fee•see•OH•nes] — (Hobbies | Spanish has different words for hobbies like "aficiones" and "pasatiempos" but the English denomination "hobbies" is also broadly used)
2. *Me gusta la fotografía* [meh GOOS•tah lah pho•toh•gra•FEE•ah] — (I like photography)
3. *Soy aficionado/a del fútbol* [SOI ah•fee•see•oh•NAH•doh/dah del FOOT•ball] — (I'm a soccer fan | *"aficionado"* for males and *"aficionada"* for females)
4. *¿Qué te gusta hacer en tu tiempo libre?* [KEH teh GOOS•tah ah•SER en too TYEM•poh LEE•breh?] — (What do you like to do in your free time?)
5. *¿Tienes algún hobby?* [TYE•nes ahl•GOON HOH•bee] — (Do you have any hobbies?)
6. *Jugar al padel* [hoo•GAR al PAH•del] — (Play padel)
7. *Tiempo libre* [TYEM•poh LEE•breh] — (Free time)
8. *Aficionado/a* [ah•fee•see•oh•NAH•doh/dah] — (Fan | use *"aficionado"* for males and *"aficionada"* for females)
9. *Fotografía* [pho•toh•gra•FEE•ah] — (Photography)
10. *En tu tiempo libre* [en too TYEM•poh LEE•breh] — (In your free time)

Planning Social Activities

The essence of social life in many Spanish-speaking cultures lies in shared experiences, from casual meet-ups to elaborate gatherings. Mastering phrases for making plans, like *"¿Quieres ir a... conmigo?"* (Do you want to go to... with me?) or *"¿Qué te parece si...?"* (How about if we...?) becomes crucial in weaving these shared moments. Whether it's *"ver una película"* (watching a movie) or *"probar un nuevo restaurante"* (trying a new restaurant), each plan is an opportunity to create memories and strengthen bonds.

Accepting invitations is equally essential, as it shows openness and eagerness to engage. *"Me encantaría"* (I would love to) or *"Claro, ¿a qué hora?"* (Sure, what time?) Not only does it convey your interest, but it also shows your willingness to immerse yourself in social dynamics. On the flip side, knowing how to decline politely, with *"Lo siento, pero ya tengo planes"* (Sorry, but I already have plans), respects the invitation while leaving the door open for future outings.

KEYWORDS/PHRASES AND HOW TO PRONOUNCE THEM:

1. *¿Quieres ir a... conmigo?* [KYEH•res eer ah... kon•MEE•goh?] — (Do you want to go to... with me?)
2. *¿Qué te parece si...?* [KEH teh pah•REH•seh see...?] — (How about if we...?)
3. *Ver una película* [behr OO•nah peh•LEE•koo•lah] — (Watching a movie)

4. *Probar un nuevo restaurante* [proh•BAR oon NWEH•vo res•tow•RAN•teh] — (Trying a new restaurant)

5. *Me encantaría* [meh en•kan•ta•REE•ah] — (I would love to)

6. *Claro, ¿a qué hora?* [KLAH•roh, ah KEH OH•rah?] — (Sure, what time?)

7. *Lo siento, pero ya tengo planes* [loh SYEN•toh, PEH•roh yah TEN•goh PLAH•nes] — (Sorry, but I already have plans.)

8. *Aceptar una invitación* [ah•sep•TAR OO•nah een•vee•ta•SYON] — (Accepting an invitation)

9. *Declinar una oferta* [deh•klee•NAR OO•nah oh•FER•tah] — (Declining an offer)

10. *Crear recuerdos* [kre•AR re•KWER•dos] — (Create memories)

Cultural Events and Festivals

Spanish-speaking countries boast an array of cultural events and festivals, each with its history, traditions, and celebrations. Being able to discuss these events, like *"La Tomatina"* in Spain or *"El Carnaval"* in various Latin American countries, reveals an interest in the culture that goes beyond surface-level engagement. *"¿Has ido alguna vez a...?"* (Have you ever gone to...?) not only seeks personal stories but also expresses a desire to understand these cultural phenomena firsthand.

For those planning to attend such events, phrases like *"Este año quiero asistir a..."* (This year I want to attend...) or *"¿Me acompañas a...?"* (Will you accompany me to...?) invite others to join in the experience, turning cultural exploration into a shared adventure. These festivals, rich in music, dance, and tradition, offer immersive experiences where language and culture intertwine, allowing for a deeper connection to local culture.

KEYWORDS/PHRASES AND HOW TO PRONOUNCE THEM:

1. *Eventos culturales* [eh•VEN•tos kool•too•RAH•les] — (Cultural events)
2. *Festivales* [fehs•tee•VAH•les] — (Festivals)
3. *La Tomatina* [lah toh•mah•TEE•nah] — (A tomato-throwing festival in Spain)
4. *El Carnaval* [ehl kar•na•VAL] — (The Carnival | celebrated in various Latin American countries)
5. *¿Has ido alguna vez a...?* [ahs EE•doh al•GOO•nah vehz ah...?] — (Have you ever gone to...?)
6. *Este año quiero asistir a...* [ES•teh AH•nyo KYEH•roh ah•sees•TEER ah...] — (This year I want to attend...)
7. *¿Me acompañas a...?* [meh ah•kom•PAH•nyas ah...?] — (Will you accompany me to...?)
8. *Tradiciones* [trah•dee•see•OH•nes] — (Traditions)
9. *Música* [MOO•see•kah] — (Music)
10. *Danza* [DAN•sah] — (Dance)

Outdoor Adventures

Spanish-speaking countries offer endless opportunities for outdoor adventures, from Caribbean's beaches to the Andes' mountains. Expressing a desire to explore these natural wonders, with *"Me gustaría hacer senderismo en..."* (I would like to go hiking in...) or *"¿Sabes dónde puedo surfear?"* (Do you know where I can surf?) shows an adventurous spirit and invites recommendations and, often, company.

Planning these excursions involves a dialogue, where phrases like *"Necesitamos llevar..."* (We need to bring...) and *"¿Cuál es la mejor época para...?"* (What's the best season for...?) Ensure preparedness and enjoyment. Whether it's a day at the beach, *"un día en la playa,"* or a mountain hike, *"una excursión a la montaña,"* these activities are more than just leisure; they're opportunities to engage with the environment, the culture, and fellow enthusiasts in meaningful ways.

Discussing and planning leisure and entertainment in Spanish does more than fill your calendar with activities; it fills your life with experiences that deepen your understanding of the culture, connect you with its people, and enrich your journey. Whether through shared hobbies, social gatherings, cultural events or outdoor adventures, each interaction weaves you deeper into the fabric of Hispanic societies, turning every moment into a thread in the vibrant tapestry of your experiences.

KEYWORDS/PHRASES AND HOW TO PRONOUNCE THEM:

1. *Me gustaría hacer senderismo en...* [meh goos•tah•REE•ah ah•SER sen•deh•REES• moh en...] — (I would like to go hiking in...)
2. *¿Sabes dónde puedo surfear?* [SAH•bes DON•deh PWEH•do sor•FEAR?] — (Do you know where I can surf?)
3. *Necesitamos llevar...* [neh•seh•see•TAH•mos yeh•VAR...] — (We need to bring...)
4. *¿Cuál es la mejor época para...?* [KWAL es lah meh•HOR EH•poh•kah PAH•rah...?] — (What's the best season for...?)
5. *Un día en la playa* [oon DEE•ah en lah PLA•yah] — (A day at the beach)
6. *Una excursión a la montaña* [OO•nah eks•kur•SYON a lah mon•TAH•nyah] — (A mountain hike)
7. *Explorar* [eks•ploh•RAR] — (To explore)
8. *Aventura al aire libre* [ah•ven•TOO•rah al AH•ee•reh LEE•breh] — (Outdoor adventure)
9. *Recomendaciones* [reh•ko•men•da•see•OH•nes] — (Recommendations)
10. *Compañía* [kom•pah•NYE•ah] — (Company | as in companionship)

Chapter 1.9 Common Spanish Phrases

1. *¿Qué te gusta hacer en tu tiempo libre? Me gusta la fotografía.* [KEH teh GOOS•tah ah•SER en too

TYEM•po LEE•breh? meh GOOS•tah lah
pho•toh•grah•FEE•ah] – (What do you like to do
in your free time? I like photography.)

2. *Soy aficionado del fútbol. ¿Quieres ir a ver un partido
conmigo?* [soi ah•fee•see•oh•NAH•doh del
FOOT•bol. KYEH•res eer ah behr oon
par•TEE•doh kon•MEE•goh?] — (I'm a soccer fan.
Do you want to go watch a game with me?)

3. *Este fin de semana hay un festival de música, ¿me
acompañas?* [ES•teh feen deh se•MAH•nah eye oon
fes•tee•VAL deh MOO•see•kah, meh
ah•kom•PAH•nyas?] — (This weekend there's a
music festival, will you accompany me?)

4. *¿Tienes algún hobby? A mí me encanta jugar al padel.*
[TYE•nes ahl•GOON HOH•bee? ah MEE meh
en•KAN•tah hoo•GAR al PAH•del] — (Do you
have any hobbies? I love to play padel.)

5. *¿Qué te parece si probamos un nuevo restaurante este
viernes?* [KEH teh pah•REH•seh see
proh•BAH•mos oon NWEH•vo res•tow•RAN•teh
ES•teh VEE•er•nes?] — (How about if we try a new
restaurant this Friday?)

6. *Lo siento, pero ya tengo planes para este sábado.* [loh
SYEN•toh, PEH•roh yah TEN•goh PLAH•nes
PAH•rah EHS•teh SAH•bah•doh] — (Sorry, but I
already have plans for this Saturday.)

7. *Me encantaría crear recuerdos yendo a eventos
culturales contigo.* [meh en•kan•ta•REE•ah kre•AR
re•KWER•dos YEN•doh ah eh•VEN•tos
kul•too•RAH•les kon•TEE•goh] — (I would love

to create memories by going to cultural events with you.)

8. *¿Has ido alguna vez a la Tomatina? Este año quiero asistir.* [ahs EE•doh ahl•GOO•nah vehz ah lah toh•mah•TEE•nah? ES•teh AH•nyo KYEH•roh ah•sees•TEER] — (Have you ever gone to La Tomatina? I want to attend this year.)

9. *Me gustaría hacer senderismo en las montañas este otoño.* [meh goos•ta•REE•ah AH•ser sen•deh•REES•mo en las mon•TAH•nyas ES•teh oh•TOH•nyo] — (I would like to go hiking in the mountains this fall.)

10. *¿Sabes dónde puedo surfear cerca de aquí?* [SAH•bes DON•deh PWEH•do sor•PHEAR SEHR•kah deh ah•KEE?] — (Do you know where I can surf around here?)

Chapter 1.9 Worksheet

Fill in the blanks with the correct Spanish terms and phrases from the following categories, using the terms and phrases discussed earlier. Good luck!

Talking about Hobbies

- Me gusta la (*photography*):

  _____

- Soy aficionado/a del (*soccer*):

  _____

- ¿Qué te gusta hacer en tu (*free time*)

  _____ libre?

- ¿Tienes algún (*hobby*)?

  _____

- Jugar al (*racket sport*):

  _____

Planning Social Activities

- ¿Quieres ir a...

  _____ conmigo?

  (*Do you want to go to the movies with me?*)
- Ver una (movie):

  _____

- Probar un nuevo (restaurant):

  _____

- Me (I would like to):

  _____

- Claro, ¿a qué

  _____? (*Sure,*

  what time?)
- Lo siento, pero ya tengo _____

  (*Sorry, but I already have plans*)

Cultural Events and Festivals

- ¿Has ido

  _____vez a...?

  (*Have you ever gone to...?*)
- Este año

  _____ asistir

  a... (*This year I want to attend...*)
- ¿

  _____acompañas

  a...? (*Will you accompany me to...?*)

Outdoor Adventures

- Me gustaría hacer

  _____ en... (*I*

  would like to go hiking in...)
- ¿Sabes dónde puedo

  _____? (*Do you*

  know where I can surf?)
- _____ llevar...

  (*We need to bring...*)
- ¿Cuál es la mejor

  _____ para...?

  (*What's the best season for...?*)
- Una día en la

  _____ (*A day at*

  the beach)
- Una excursión a la

  _____ (*A*

  mountain hike)

2) **Dialogue:** Ana and Carlos discuss attending a soccer game, their interest in festivals, the possibility of surfing, and what they need to have fun.

Ana: *Hola Carlos, ¿qué te gusta hacer?*
[O•lah Carlos, KEH teh GOOS•tah ah•SER?]
(Hello Carlos, what do you like to do?)

Carlos: *Hola Ana, me gusta ver fútbol.*
[O•lah Ana, meh GOOS•tah vehr FOOT•bol.]
(Hi Ana, I like to watch soccer.)

Ana: *¿Vamos juntos a un partido?*
[VAH•mohs HOON•tohs ah oon pahr•TEE•doh?]
(Shall we go to a game together?)

Carlos: *Sí, ¿a qué hora?*
[SEE, ah KEH O•rah?]
(Yes, what time?)

Ana: *A las tres.*
[ah lahs trehs.]
(At three.)

Carlos: *¡Perfecto!*
[pehr•FEHK•toh!]
(Perfect!)

Ana: *¿Has ido a festivales aquí?*
[ahs EE•doh ah fes•tee•VAH•lehs ah•KEE?]
(Have you been to festivals here?)

Carlos: No, pero quiero ir.
[noh, PEH•roh KYEH•roh eer.]
(No, but I want to go.)

Ana: *Puedes surfear también.*
[PWE•dehs sor•PHEAR tahn•BYEHN.]
(You can also surf.)

Carlos: *¿Dónde?*
[DOHN•deh?]
(Where?)

Ana: *En la playa cerca.*
[ehn lah PLA•yah SEHR•kah.]
(At the beach nearby.)

Carlos: *¿Qué necesitamos?*
[keh neh•seh•see•TAH•mohs?]
(What do we need?)

Ana: *Solo ganas de divertirnos.*
[SOH•loh GAH•nahs deh dee•vehr•TEER•nos.]
(Just a desire to have fun.)

1.10 Family and Relationships: Conversing with Loved Ones

Family and personal relationships lie at the heart of Hispanic cultures, often shaping social interactions and the fabric of daily life. The Spanish language reflects this importance, offering rich and varied ways to express familial bonds, emotions, and the nuances of relationships.

Family Terms

Navigating the vocabulary surrounding family members is a fundamental aspect of conversing in Spanish. Family, *"la familia,"* extends beyond the immediate *"núcleo familiar"* to include many relatives. For instance, *"padres"* means parents, while *"madre"* and *"padre"* distinguish between mother and father. Siblings are *"hermanos,"* with *"hermana"* and *"hermano"* specifying sister and brother, respectively.

The extended family plays a significant role, and Spanish also provides terms for these relations. *"Abuelos"* refers to grandparents, splitting into *"abuela"* for grandmother and *"abuelo"* for grandfather. Aunts and uncles are *"tías"* and *"tíos,"* while cousins are collectively known as *"primos,"* differentiating into *"prima"* for female and *"primo"* for male cousins.

Discussing family often leads to sharing stories and traditions, enriching the dialogue with personal history and cultural insights. For those with children, *"hijos"* denotes children, with *"hija"* and *"hijo"* for daughter and son. These terms not only label family members but also weave the tapestry of one's familial landscape, painting a picture of life's interconnectedness.

KEYWORDS/PHRASES AND HOW TO PRONOUNCE THEM:

1. *La familia* [lah fah•MEE•lee•ah] — (The family)
2. *Núcleo familiar* [NOO•kleh•oh fah•mee•lee•AHR] — (Immediate family)

3. *Padres* [PAH•dres] — (Parents)
4. *Madre* [MAH•dreh] — (Mother)
5. *Padre* [PAH•dreh] — (Father)
6. *Hermanos* [err•MAH•nos] — (Siblings)
7. *Hermana* [err•MAH•nah] — (Sister)
8. *Hermano* [err•MAH•noh] — (Brother)
9. *Abuelos* [ah•BWEH•los] — (Grandparents)
10. *Abuela* [ah•BWEH•lah] — (Grandmother)
11. *Abuelo* [ah•BWEH•loh] — (Grandfather)
12. *Tías* [TEE•ahs] — (Aunts)
13. *Tíos* [TEE•ohs] — (Uncles)
14. *Primos* [PREE•mos] — (Cousins)
15. *Prima* [PREE•mah] — (Female cousin)
16. *Primo* [PREE•moh] — (Male cousin)
17. *Hijos* [EE•hos] — Children
18. *Hija* [EE•hah] — Daughter
19. *Hijo* [EE•hoh] — Son

Describing People and Personalities

Describing loved ones goes beyond their role in the family, you might also delve into the physical attributes and personality traits that make each person unique. Physical descriptions utilize a range of adjectives, such as "*alto*" (tall), "*bajo*" (short), "*joven*" (young) and "*viejo*" (old), alongside hair and eye color — "*pelo rubio*" (blonde hair), "*ojos azules*" (blue eyes), for instance. These descriptions often accompany stories or introductions, providing a vivid image of the discussed person.

On the other hand, personality traits delve deeper into what makes a person who they are. Describing someone as *"amable"* (kind), *"gracioso"* (funny) or *"serio"* (serious) touches on their demeanor and how they interact with the world. Conversations might explore someone's nature further with phrases like *"Él es muy trabajador"* (He is very hardworking) or *"Ella es bastante aventurera"* (She is quite adventurous), offering glimpses into individual characters and life philosophies.

KEYWORDS/PHRASES AND HOW TO PRONOUNCE THEM:

1. *Alto* [AHL•toh] — (Tall)
2. *Bajo* [BAH•ho] — (Short)
3. *Joven* [HOH•ven] — (Young)
4. *Viejo* [VYEH•hoh] — (Old)
5. *Pelo rubio* [PEH•loh ROO•byo] — (Blonde hair)
6. *Ojos azules* [O•hos ah•ZOO•les] — (Blue eyes)
7. *Amable* [ah•MAH•bleh] — (Kind)
8. *Gracioso* [grah•see•OH•so] — (Funny)
9. *Serio* [SEH•ryo] — (Serious)
10. *Él es muy trabajador* [EHL ehs MOO•ee trah•bah•hah•DOHR] — (He is very hardworking)
11. *Ella es bastante aventurera* [EH•yah ehs bahs•TAHN•teh ah•ven•too•REH•rah] — (She is quite adventurous.)

Stages of Life and Celebrations

Critical life events and milestones are universal, yet each culture celebrates these moments with unique customs and expressions. In Spanish, there's a rich vocabulary for marking these occasions, from *"cumpleaños"* (birthdays) to *"bodas"* (weddings) and *"aniversarios"* (anniversaries). Expressing congratulations, *"Felicitaciones,"* or offering best wishes, *"Los mejores deseos,"* are common goodwill gestures during these celebrations.

Significant stages, such as graduation *"graduación,"* new jobs *"nuevo trabajo,"* or retirements *"jubilación,"* are recognized and celebrated within the family and community. Phrases like *"Estoy orgulloso/a de ti"* (I'm proud of you) convey support and pride, strengthening bonds and acknowledging achievements.

Conversely, during times of loss or sorrow, offering condolences, *"Mis condolencias"* and support *"Estoy aquí para lo que necesites"* (I'm here for whatever you need), is crucial. These expressions of empathy and solidarity provide comfort, showcasing the language's capacity to convey care and compassion.

KEYWORDS/PHRASES AND HOW TO PRONOUNCE THEM:

1. *Cumpleaños* [koom•pleh•AH•nyos] — (Birthdays)
2. *Bodas* [BOH•dahs] — (Weddings)
3. *Aniversarios* [ah•nee•ver•SAH•ryos] — (Anniversaries)

4. *Felicitaciones* [feh•lee•see•tah•SYOH•nes] —
   (Congratulations)
5. *Los mejores deseos* [lohs meh•HOH•res
   deh•SEH•os] — (Best wishes)
6. *Graduación* [grah•doo•ah•SYON] — (Graduation)
7. *Nuevo trabajo* [NWE•voh trah•BAH•ho] —
   (New job)
8. *Jubilación* [hoo•bee•lah•SYON] — (Retirement)
9. *Estoy orgulloso/a de ti* [es•TOI or•goo•YOH•soh/ah
   deh tee] — (I'm proud of you | use *"orgulloso"* for
   male and *"orgullosa"* for female)
10. *Mis condolencias* [mees kon•doh•LEN•syahs] —
    (My condolences)
11. *Estoy aquí para lo que necesites* [es•TOI ah•KEE
    PAH•rah loh keh neh•seh•SEE•tes] — (I'm here for
    whatever you need)

Cultural Norms around Relationships

Understanding the cultural norms surrounding relationships in Spanish-speaking societies adds depth to interactions, revealing the values and expectations that guide social
behavior. Terms of endearment, for instance, play a significant role in expressing affection. *"Querido"* (dear) or *"amor"*
(love) are commonly used, not just in romantic contexts but
also among close friends and family, underscoring the
warmth and affection prevalent in these cultures.

Addressing others respectfully is paramount, particularly in
formal or less familiar settings. Using *"usted"* instead of *"tú"*
in specific contexts signifies respect and distance, a nuance

important in maintaining proper social etiquette. However, transitioning from "*usted*" to "*tú*" can deepen the relationship, moving from formal to more intimate grounds.

Family and community are intertwined in many Hispanic cultures, with collective gatherings and inclusive social circles being the norm. Invitations to homes, "*invitaciones a casas,*" are not just casual offers but are extended with genuine hospitality. The phrase "*Mi casa es tu casa*" (My home is your home) epitomizes this open-hearted approach, encapsulating an essence of community.

Navigating the complexities of family and relationships in Spanish involves more than mastering vocabulary; it's about understanding the cultural currents that shape these expressions. From celebrating life's milestones to offering support in times of need, the language serves as a conduit for sharing experiences, emotions, and values. It fosters connections that transcend linguistic barriers, embedding one more profound into the rich tapestry of Spanish-speaking cultures, where family and relationships are cherished pillars of daily life.

KEYWORDS/PHRASES AND HOW TO PRONOUNCE THEM:

1. *Querido/Querida* [keh•REE•doh/dah] — (Dear | masculine/feminine)
2. *Amor* [ah•MOR] — (Love)
3. *Usted* [oos•TEHD] — (You | formal)
4. *Tú* [TOO] — (You | informal)

5. *Invitaciones a casas* [in•vee•tah•SYO•nes ah
   KAH•sahs] — (Invitations to homes)
6. *Mi casa es tu casa* [mee KAH•sah es too KAH•sah]
   — (My home is your home)
7. *Respeto* [res•PEH•toh] — (Respect)
8. *Familia* [fah•MEE•lyah] — (Family)
9. *Comunidad* [koh•moo•nee•DAHD] —
   (Community)
10. *Hospitalidad* [os•pee•tah•lee•DAHD] —
    (Hospitality)

Chapter 1.10 Common Spanish Phrases

1. *Mi familia es el núcleo de mi vida.* [mee
   fah•MEE•lee•ah es el NOO•kleh•oh de mee
   vee•dah] — (My family is the core of my life.)
2. *Mis padres son amables y trabajadores.* [mees
   PAH•dres son AH•mah•blehs y
   trah•bah•hah•DOH•res] — (My parents are kind
   and hardworking.)
3. *Tengo dos hermanos, un hermano y una hermana.*
   [TEN•go dos err•MAH•nos, oon err•MAH•noh y
   OO•nah err•MAH•nah] — (I have two siblings, one
   brother and one sister.)
4. *Mi abuelo tiene ojos azules y pelo rubio.* [mee
   ah•BWEH•loh tee•EH•neh OH•hos AH•zoo•les y
   PEH•loh ROO•byo] — (My grandfather has blue
   eyes and blonde hair.)
5. *Celebramos los cumpleaños en familia.*
   [seh•leh•BRAH•mos los koom•pleh•AH•nyos en

fah•MEE•lee•ah] — (We celebrate birthdays with the family.)

6. *Mi prima es joven y bastante aventurera.* [mee PREE•mah es HOH•ven y bahs•TAN•teh ah•ven•too•REH•rah] — (My female cousin is young and quite adventurous.)

7. *Estoy orgulloso de mi hijo por graduarse.* [es•TOI or•goo•YOH•soh deh mee EE•hoh por grah•doo•AHR•seh] — (I'm proud of my son for graduating.)

8. *Este fin de semana vamos a una boda.* [ES•teh feen deh se•MAH•nah VAH•mos ah OO•nah BOH•dah] — (This weekend we are going to a wedding.)

9. *Mi hermana mayor se jubiló el año pasado.* [mee err•MAH•nah mah•YOR seh hoo•bee•LOH el AH•nyo pah•SA•doh] — (My older sister retired last year.)

10. *Mi casa es tu casa cuando quieras visitar.* [mee KAH•sah es too KAH•sah KWAN•doh KYEH•ras vee•see•TAHR] — (My home is your home whenever you want to visit.)

Chapter 1.10 Worksheet

Fill in the blanks with the correct Spanish terms and phrases from the following categories: family terms, describing people and personalities, stages of life and celebrations, and cultural norms around relationships. Refer to the terms and phrases provided previously.

Family Terms

- La _____ es el
  núcleo de la sociedad. (*Family is the core of society.*)
- Los _____
  (*grandparents*) son a menudo el corazón de la
  familia.
- Una _____
  (*wedding*) es un evento donde se reúnen todos los
  miembros de la familia.

Describing People and Personalities

- Ella es muy
  _____ (*friendly*),
  siempre saluda a todos con una sonrisa.
- Mi tío es el más
  _____
  (*hardworking*) de la familia.
- Mi mejor amigo es muy
  _____ (*funny*), siempre sabe
  cómo hacerme reír.

Stages of Life and Celebrations

- Cada _____
  (*birthday*) es una celebración de la vida.
- La _____
  (*graduation*) marca el final de una etapa y el
  comienzo de otra.

- En una _____
  (*retirement*), celebramos los años de trabajo y
  esfuerzo.

Cultural Norms around Relationships

- Cuando visitas a alguien, es común decir (*my home
  is your home*): _____
- El respeto es importante, y por eso usamos
  _____ (*formal
  you*) con personas mayores.
- En una relación cercana, es más común usar
  (*informal you*): _____

2) **Dialogue:** Follow the conversation of two people who are
planning to meet at a family event.

Juan: *Hola, Sofia, ¿cómo estás?*
[O•lah, Sofía, KOH•moh es•TAHS?]
(Hello Sofia, how are you?)

Sofia: *Hola, Juan, estoy bien, ¿y tú?*
[O•lah, Juan, es•TOI BYEN, ee TOO?]
(Hello Juan, I am well, and you?)

Juan: *Bien también. ¿Vas a la fiesta de abuela mañana?*
[byen tahm•BYEN. VAHS ah lah FYEHS•tah deh
ah•BWE•lah mah•NYAH•nah?]
(Good, too. Are you going to grandma's party tomorrow?)

Sofia: *Sí, voy con toda la familia. Será divertido.*
[SEE, voi kohn TOH•dah lah fah•MEE•lee•ah. seh•RAH
dee•vehr•TEE•doh.]
(Yes, I am going with the whole family. It will be fun.)

Juan: *¿Cuántos años cumple la abuela?*
[KWAN•tos AH•nyos KOOM•ple lah ah•BWE•lah?)
(How old is grandma turning?)

Sofia: *Cumple setenta años.*
[KOOM•ple seh•TEHN•tah AH•nyos.)
(She is turning seventy years old.)

Juan: *¡Qué grande! Debo comprar un regalo.*
[KEH GRAHN•deh! DEH•bo kom•PRAR oon
reh•GAH•lo.]
(How great! I should buy a gift.)

Sofia: *Ella ama las flores.*
[EH•yah AH•mah lahs FLOH•res.]
(She loves flowers.)

Juan: *Bueno, compraré flores para ella.*
[BWEH•noh, kom•pra•REH FLOH•res PAH•ra EH•yah.]
(Well, I will buy flowers for her.)

Sofia: *Y yo haré una tarjeta.*
[ee yo ah•REH OO•nah TAR•heh•tah.]
(And I will make a card.)

Juan: *Es una buena idea. La abuela estará feliz.*
[ehs OO•nah BWEH•nah ee•DEH•ah. lah ah•BWE•lah
es•tah•RAH feh•LEES.]
(That's a good idea. Grandma will be happy.)

Sofia: *Sí, la familia es importante.*
[SEE, lah fah•MEE•lee•ah es eem•por•TAHN•teh.]
(Yes, family is important.)

Make a Difference with Your Review

Unlock the Power of Generosity

"Money can't buy happiness, but giving it away can."

Freddie Mercury

Hola, amigos y amigas! Did you know that people who give without expecting anything in return tend to lead happier, more fulfilling lives? Well, if there's a chance to experience that joy together, let's grab it with both hands!

I have a very important question for you...

Would you be willing to help someone you've never met, even if you don't get a shoutout for it?

Who is this mystery person, you might wonder? Well, they're a lot like you once were—eager to learn Spanish, ready to explore new cultures, and looking for a little guidance on where to start.

Our goal with "Beginner's Spanish for Adults: Speak Spanish Rapidly: Master Language & Travel Essentials: 2-in-1 Adult Guide - BOOK 1" is to make learning this beautiful language accessible to everyone. Everything I do is driven by this mission. And to truly succeed, I need to reach... well, everyone!

That's where your help comes in. It turns out, a lot of people do judge a book by its cover—or, more specifically, by its reviews. So here's my request on behalf of a future Spanish speaker you've never met:

Could you please take a moment to leave a review for this book?

It won't cost you a dime and will take less than a minute, but your words could have a lifelong impact on another learner. Your review could help:

- ...one more small business thrive in its community.
- ...one more entrepreneur support their family.
- ...one more worker find meaningful employment.
- ...one more client change their life.
- ...one more dream come true.

To share your thoughts and spread the joy of learning, just scan the QR code below:

If the idea of helping a fellow Spanish learner excites you, then you're definitely my kind of person! Welcome to our community of passionate learners.

I'm incredibly excited to continue helping you enhance your Spanish skills. You're going to love the practical tips and strategies in the upcoming chapters.

Thank you from the bottom of my heart for your support and generosity.

- Your biggest fan,

Austin Fultz

P.S. - Remember, when you offer value to someone else, you increase your own value in their eyes. If you believe this book can help another beginner, why not share it and spread the goodwill?

TWO

Cultural Immersion from Your Couch

I magine you've just landed in a bustling Spanish-speaking city, your senses immediately engulfed by new sights, sounds and aromas. Now, picture this sensory overload magnified during a local festival, where the air is thick with anticipation and the streets come alive with color and music. This chapter is your ticket to understanding and participating in these celebrations, a way to immerse yourself in the rich cultural fabric of Hispanic countries without stepping outside your door. By exploring celebrations and holidays, you'll learn new vocabulary and gain insights into the customs and traditions that define these vibrant communities. So, let's lace up our metaphorical dancing shoes and join the festivities.

2.1 Celebrations and Holidays: Join in the Festivities

Understanding Cultural Significance

Each festival and holiday in the Spanish-speaking world carries layers of meaning rooted in history, religion and local customs. Take *"Día de los Muertos,"* a Mexican celebration that honors deceased loved ones, blending indigenous Aztec rituals with Catholic traditions. Understanding the significance behind altars, *"ofrendas,"* and the marigolds, *"cempasúchil,"* opens up a nuanced appreciation of this profound celebration. Similarly, "La Tomatina," a seemingly whimsical tomato-throwing festivity from Spain, stems from a spontaneous act of local youths in 1945, evolving into a symbol of joy and community spirit. Delving into the stories behind these celebrations enriches your cultural vocabulary, connecting you to these societies more profoundly.

Key vocabulary for celebrations

- *Fiesta* [fee•ES•tah] — (Party/Celebration): The umbrella term for any festive gathering, from birthdays to national holidays.
- *Desfile* [des•FEE•leh] — (Parade): A common feature in many celebrations, showcasing elaborate floats and costumes.
- *Fuegos artificiales* [foo•EH•gos ar•tee•fee•cee•A•les] — (Fireworks): A spectacle of light and sound that marks the climax of many festivals.

- *Máscaras* [MAS•ca•ras] – (Masks) and *Disfraces* [dees•frA•ces] – (Costumes): are essential elements in celebrations like Carnival, embodying transformation and festivity.

Incorporating these terms into your lexicon boosts your language skills and prepares you to participate in these events, whether as an observer or an active participant.

Discussing plans to attend or host events is a practical exercise when immersing in a new language. Phrases like *"¿Vamos al desfile juntos?"* (Shall we go to the parade together?) or *"Necesitamos preparar la comida para la fiesta"* (We need to prepare the food for the party) are key in order to get involved in the celebration and its planning. Advice on what to wear, *"qué ponerse,"* or what to bring, *"qué traer,"* hinges on understanding the nature of the event, whether it's a formal *"cena"* (dinner) or a casual *"reunión"* (gathering). This practical language application bridges cultural knowledge with real-life interactions.

KEYWORDS/PHRASES AND HOW TO PRONOUNCE THEM:

1. *Fiesta* [FYES•tah] — (Party/Celebration)
2. *Día de los Muertos* [dEE•ah deh lohs MWER•tos] — (Day of the Dead | A Mexican celebration that honors deceased loved ones)
3. *Ofrendas* [oh•FREN•dahs] — (Offerings | Altars with offerings for the deceased during Día de los Muertos)

4. *Cempasúchil* [sem•pah•SOO•cheel] — (Marigolds | Flowers used to decorate the ofrendas on Día de los Muertos, symbolizing death and the sun)
5. *La Tomatina* [lah toh•mah•TEE•nah] — (Tomato Fight Festival | A festival in Buñol, Spain, where participants throw tomatoes at each other)
6. *Desfile* [dehs•FEE•leh] — (Parade)
7. *Fuegos artificiales* [FWE•gos ar•tee•fEE•see•ah•les] — (Fireworks)
8. *Máscaras* [MAS•kah•ras] — (Masks)
9. *Disfraces* [dees•FRAH•ses] — (Costumes)
10. *Cena* [SEH•nah] — (Dinner)
11. *Reunión* [reh•oo•nee•On] — (Gathering)
12. *¿Vamos al desfile juntos?* [VAH•mos al dehs•FEE•leh HOON•tos] — (Shall we go to the parade together?)
13. *Necesitamos preparar la comida para la fiesta* [neh•seh•see•TAH•mos preh•pah•RAHR lah co•MEE•da PAH•rah lah FYES•tah] — (We need to prepare the food for the party)
14. *Qué ponerse* [KEH poh•NER•seh] — (What to wear)
15. *Qué traer* [kEh tra•EHR] — (What to bring)

Cultural Etiquette and Customs

Navigating the do's and don'ts during these celebrations ensures respectful and enjoyable participation. For instance, during "Semana Santa" (Holy Week), a time of solemn processions and religious observance, understanding the tone and activities appropriate for this period fosters a deeper connection with its significance. On the other hand, knowing the playful yet respectful approach to "Carnaval" allows total immersion in its exuberant festivities without overstepping boundaries.

Tips for respectful participation:

- Always ask before taking photos, especially during ceremonies or private events.
- Dress appropriately, considering the event's nature, local customs and weather.
- Participate actively when invited, whether it's dancing at a "fiesta" or attending a "misa" (mass) during religious holidays.

By embracing celebrations with an open heart and a keen understanding of their cultural significance, you enrich your language skills and forge lasting memories and connections. The joy of shared experiences transcends linguistic barriers, allowing you an authentic immersion into Spanish-speaking cultures. Through the lens of celebrations and holidays, language becomes a living, breathing entity pulsating with the rhythms of life itself.

KEYWORDS/PHRASES AND HOW TO PRONOUNCE THEM:

1. *Semana Santa* [se•MAH•nah SAN•tah] — (Holy Week)
2. *Procesiones* [proh•seh•see•OH•nes] — (Processions)
3. *Respeto* [res•PEH•toh] — (Respect)
4. *Misa* [MEE•sah] — (Mass)

5. *Vestimenta adecuada* [ves•tee•MEN•tah
ah•deh•KWAh•dah] — (Appropriate dress)

6. *Permiso para tomar fotos* [per•MEE•soh PAH•rah
to•MAR FOH•tos] — (Permission to take photos)

7. *Participar activamente* [par•tee•see•PAR
ak•TEE•vah•men•teh] — (Participate actively)

8. *Inmersión cultural* [een•mer•see•ON KUL•too•ral]
— (Cultural immersion)

Chapter 2.1 Common Spanish Phrases

1. *Vamos a hacer ofrendas para el Día de los Muertos*
[VAH•mos ah ah•CER oh•FREN•dahs PAH•rah el
DEE•ah deh lohs MWER•tos] — (We're going to
make offerings for the Day of the Dead)

2. *La fiesta incluirá fuegos artificiales a medianoche* [lah
FYES•tah een•kloo•ee•RAH FWE•gos
ar•tee•fee•see•AH•les ah meh•dee•ah•NOH•che]
— (The party will include fireworks at midnight)

3. *¿Te gustaría venir a la cena con nosotros?* [teh
goos•ta•REE•ah veh•NEER ah lah SEH•nah kon
no•SO•tros] — (Would you like to come to dinner
with us?)

4. *En Semana Santa, hay muchas procesiones en la
ciudad* [en se•MAH•nah SAN•tah eye MOO•chas
proh•seh•see•OH•nes en la see•oo•DAD] — (For
Holy Week, there are many processions in the city)

5. *Usaremos máscaras y disfraces para el carnaval*
[oo•sah•REH•mos MAS•ka•ras ee
dees•FRAH•ses PAH•rah el kar•na•VAL] — (We'll
wear masks and costumes for the carnival)

6. *La Tomatina es una fiesta única en España* [lah toh•mah•TEE•nah es OO•nah FYES•tah OO•nee•kah en es•PAH•nyah] — (La Tomatina is a unique celebration in Spain)

7. *Todos debemos llevar vestimenta adecuada a la misa* [TOH•dos deh•BEH•mos yeh•VAR ves•tee•MEN•tah ah•deh•KWA•dah a lah MEE•sah] — (Everyone should wear appropriate dress to the mass)

8. *¿Qué traer para la ofrenda de Día de los Muertos?* [KEH tra•ER PAH•rah oh•FREN•dah deh DEE•ah de lohs MWER•tos?] — What to bring for the Day of the Dead offering?)

9. *Es importante participar activamente y con respeto en las procesiones* [es eem•por•TAN•teh par•tee•see•PAR ak•TEE•vah•men•teh ee kon res•PEH•toh en las proh•seh•see•OH•nes] — (During Holy Week, the community comes together in prayer)

Chapter 2.1 Worksheet

1) Use the Spanish terms and phrases provided below to fill in the blanks related to cultural etiquette and customs, planning and attending events, and understanding cultural significance.

Cultural etiquette and customs:

_____

Planning events:

_____

Attending events:

_____

Understanding cultural significance:

_____

Greeting and goodbyes:

_____

Table manners:

_____

Gift giving:

_____

Punctuality:

_____

Respect for elders:

_____

Business etiquette:

_____

2) Dialogue: The conversation below keeps the sentences short and the vocabulary basic, making it more approachable for someone just starting to learn Spanish. It introduces key concepts about *Día de los Muertos* in an informative but not overwhelming way.

—**Juan:** *Hola, María. ¿Vas a la fiesta de Día de los Muertos?*
[O•lah, mah•REE•ah. vahs ah lah fee•ES•tah deh DEE•ah deh los MWER•tos?]
(Hello, Maria. Are you going to the Day of the Dead party?)

—**Maria:** *Hola, Juan. Sí, voy a ir. Es importante recordar a la familia.*
[O•lah, hWAhn. SEE, voy ah eer. es eem•por•TAHN•teh reh•kor•DAR ah lah fah•MEE•lee•ah]
(Hello, Juan. Yes, I am going. It is important to remember the family)

—**Juan:** *¿Qué llevas al altar?*
[KEH YEH•vahs ahl al•TAR?]
(What are you bringing to the altar?)

—**Maria:** *Llevo flores y comida que le gustaba a mi abuelo.*
[YEH•voh FLOH•res ee koh•MEE•dah keh leh goos•TAH•bah ah mee ah•BWEH•loh]
(I am bringing flowers and food that my grandfather liked)

—**Juan:** *Yo llevo velas y una foto.*
[yo YEH•voh VEH•lahs ee OO•nah FOH•toh]
(I am bringing candles and a photo)

—**Maria:** *Es un día para celebrar y recordar.*
[es oon DEE•ah PAH•rah seh•leh•BRAHR ee reh•kor•DAR]

(It is a day to celebrate and remember)

—**Juan:** *Vamos con respeto y alegría.*
[VAH•mohs kon rehs•PEH•toh ee ah•leh•GREE•ah]
(We go with respect and joy)

—**Maria:** *Sí, es una tradición muy bonita.*
[SEE, es OO•nah trah•dee•see•ON MOO•ee
boh•NEE•tah]
(Yes, it is a very beautiful tradition)

2.2 Music and Movies: Improving Your Spanish with Pop Culture

Music and cinema are two of the greatest tools for language learning and cultural immersion. This section invites you to explore the rhythm and narratives that define these communities, from heart-thumping beats to poignant cinematic tales.

Popular Genres and Artists

The music scene in Spanish-speaking countries is as diverse as the regions, each genre echoing stories of love, struggle, and celebration. **Latin Pop**, a fusion of traditional and contemporary sounds, captivates with its catchy melodies and universal themes. Artists like **Shakira** and **Enrique Iglesias** have brought Latin pop to global audiences, blending languages and cultures in their tunes.

Reggaeton, originating from the streets of Puerto Rico, pulses with its distinctive dembow rhythm. Acts such as **Daddy Yankee** and **Bad Bunny** have propelled this genre to international fame, narrating tales of life, resistance and partying in their lyrics. Meanwhile, **Salsa** offers a more traditional rhythm, inviting dancers to the floor with its vibrant, intricate patterns. Artists like **Celia Cruz** and **Marc Anthony** continue influencing new generations with their timeless sounds.

Exploring these genres enhances your vocabulary and understanding of the cultural contexts that shape these musical narratives. Creating playlists of favorite tracks and artists becomes an immersive language lesson, with each song a story waiting to be understood.

KEYWORDS/PHRASES AND HOW TO PRONOUNCE THEM:

1. *Música latina* [MOO•see•kah lah•TEE•nah] — (Latin music)
2. *Pop latino* [pop lah•TEE•noh] — (Latin pop)
3. *Melodías pegajosas* [meh•loh•DEE•as peh•gah•HOH•sas] — (Catchy melodies)
4. *Temas universales* [TEH•mas oo•nee•vehr•SAH•lehs] — (Universal themes)
5. *Reggaetón* [reh•gueh•TON — (Reggaeton)
6. *Ritmo Dembow* [REET•mo dehm•bOW] — (Dembow Rhythm)
7. *Fama internacional* [FAH•mah een•ter•na•see•o•NAL] — (International fame)
8. *Salsa* [SAHL•sa] — (Salsa)

9. *Patrones intrincados* [pah•TROH•nes een•tree•KAH•dohs] — (Intricate patterns)
10. *Influencia generacional* [een•floo•EHN•see•ah heh•ne•RAH•see•o•nal] — (Generational influence)

Film and Television for Language Learning

Hispanic cinema and television present an array of genres, from gripping dramas to whimsical comedies, each providing insights into societal values and struggles. Movies like *Pan's Labyrinth* (2006) and *The Secret in Their Eyes* (2009) showcase the depth of storytelling and historical layers. At the same time, series such as *Money Heist* and *Elite* offer contemporary views of Spanish society.

For language learners, films and TV shows serve as tools for enhancing listening skills and understanding cultural nuances—subtitles in Spanish aid comprehension, allowing you to match spoken words with text. Recommendations for must-watch content often include classics and contemporary hits, providing a range of linguistic and thematic experiences.

Engaging with these media forms goes beyond passive watching. Note-taking on new vocabulary, pausing to replay complex dialogues, and discussing plotlines are active strategies that turn entertainment into education. Film clubs or discussion groups can further deepen this engagement, offering platforms for conversation and critique.

KEYWORDS/PHRASES AND HOW TO PRONOUNCE THEM:

1. *Cine* [SEE•neh] — (Cinema)
2. *Televisión* [teh•leh•vee•see•ON] — (Television)
3. *Géneros* [HEH•ne•ros] — (Genres)
4. *Comedias* [ko•MEH•dee•as] — (Comedies)
5. *Valores Sociales* [vah•LOH•res so•see•A•les] — (Social Values)
6. *Lucha Social* [LOO•cha so•see•AL] — (Societal Struggle)
7. *Narración* [nah•rrah•see•ON] — (Storytelling)
8. *Capas Históricas* [KA•pas ees•TO•ree•kas] — (Historical Layers)
9. *Subtítulos* [soob•TEE•too•los] — (Subtitles)
10. *Comprensión* [kom•pren•see•ON] — (Comprehension)

Discussing Preferences and Critiques

Expressing opinions on music and films enriches conversations and fosters connections. Phrases like *"Me encanta la música de..."* (I love the music of...) or *"La película fue impresionante debido a..."* (The movie was impressive because of...) enable you to share your tastes and insights. Dislikes and critiques also form part of this dialogue, with constructions such as *"No me gustó el final de..."* (I didn't like the ending of...) or *"La actuación fue débil en..."* (The acting was weak in...) offering balance to discussions.

This exchange of opinions, not only practices language use but also hones critical thinking in Spanish. You are preparing to defend your views or explore differing perspectives, challenging you to articulate thoughts and expanding your linguistic and analytical skills.

KEYWORDS/PHRASES AND HOW TO PRONOUNCE THEM:

1. *Expresar opiniones* [eks•preh•SAR o•pee•NYOHN•nes] — (Expressing opinions)
2. *Me encanta la música de...* [meh en•KAHN•tah lah MOO•see•kah deh...] — (I love the music of...)
3. *La película fue impresionante* [lah peh•LEE•koo•lah fwee im•pres•ee•o•NAN•teh] — (The movie was impressive)
4. *Debido a...* [deh•BEE•doh ah...] — (Because of...)
5. *No me gustó* [noh meh goos•TOH] — (I didn't like)
6. *El final de...* [el fee•NAHL deh...] — (The ending of...)
7. *La actuación fue débil* [lah ahk•too•ah•see•OHN fwee DEH•beel] — (The acting was weak)
8. *Conexiones* [ko•nek•see•OHN•ehs] — (Connections)
9. *Gustos e insights* [GOOS•tohs eh insights] — (Tastes and insights)
10. *Críticas* [KREE•tee•kahs] — (Critiques)
11. *Pensamiento crítico* [pen•sah•mee•EHN-toh KREE•tee•koh] — (Critical thinking)
12. *Defender tus puntos de vista* [deh•fen•DER toos

POON•tos deh VEES•tah] — (Defend your points of view)

13. *Perspectivas diferentes* [per•spek•TEE•vahs dee•feh•REN•tehs] — (Different perspectives)

14. *Articular pensamientos* [ar•tee•koo•LAR pen•sah•mee•EHN•tos] — (Articulate thoughts)

15. *Habilidades lingüísticas y analíticas* [ah•bee•lee•DAH•des leen•GWEES•tee•kahs ee ah•nah•LEE•tee•kahs] — (Linguistic and analytical skills)

Cultural Themes in Media

Diving into the cultural themes in Spanish-speaking media reveals much about societal values, struggles, and humor. Many films and songs grapple with themes of identity, migration and resistance, reflecting the complexities of modern life in these communities. Humor, often laced with satire and wit, serves as a coping mechanism and a mirror to societal quirks and contradictions.

Understanding these themes requires not only language proficiency but also cultural sensitivity. Recognizing the historical and social contexts that shape these narratives allows for a deeper appreciation of the content, transforming entertainment into a rich educational experience.

In essence, immersing yourself in the music and movies of Spanish-speaking cultures offers a joyful and profound route to language mastery. Each song and film becomes a lesson in vocabulary, listening, and cultural understanding, proving that entertainment and education can go hand in hand.

KEYWORDS/PHRASES AND HOW TO PRONOUNCE THEM:

1. *Temas culturales* [TE•mas kul•too•RA•les] — (Cultural themes)
2. *Valores sociales* [vah•LOH•res so•see•Ah•les] — (Societal values)
3. *Lucha social* [LOO•cha so•see•AL] — (Social struggle)
4. *Humor* [oo•MOR] — (Humor)
5. *Identidad* [ee•den•tee•DAHD] — (Identity)
6. *Migración* [mee•grah•see•OHN] — (Migration)
7. *Resistencia* [res•ees•TEN•see•ah] — (Resistance)
8. *Sátira* [SA•tee•ra] — (Satire)
9. *Sensibilidad cultural* [sen•see•bee•lee•DAHD kul•too•RAL] — (Cultural sensitivity)
10. *Contextos históricos y sociales* [kon•TEKS•tos ees•TO•ree•kos ee so•see•AH•les] — (Historical and social contexts)
11. *Apreciación* [ah•preh•see•ah•see•OHN] — (Appreciation)
12. *Entretenimiento* [en•tre•teh•nee•mee•EN•to] — (Entertainment)
13. *Experiencia educativa* [eks•peh•ree•EN•see•ah eh•doo•kah•TEE•vah] — (Educational experience)
14. *Música* [MOO•see•kah]— (Music)
15. *Películas* [peh•LEE•koo•las] — (Movies)

Chapter 2.2 Common Spanish Phrases

1. *Me encanta el reggaetón por sus melodías pegajosas.*
   [meh en•KAHN•tah el reh•gueh•TOHN por soos
   meh•loh•DEE•ahs peh•gah•HOH•sahs] — (I love
   reggaeton for its catchy melodies)

2. *La película fue impresionante por sus capas históricas.*
   [lah peh•LEE•koo•lah fwee
   im•pres•ee•oh•NAHN•teh por soos KAH•pahs
   ees•TOH•ree•kahs] — (The movie was impressive
   for its historical layers)

3. *Las comedias a menudo reflejan valores sociales y lucha
   social.* [lahs ko•MEH•dee•ahs ah meh•NOO•doh
   reh•FLEH•han vah•LOH•res so•see•AH•les ee
   LOO•cha so•see•AL] — (Comedies often reflect
   social values and societal struggles)

4. *Debido a su fama internacional, la salsa es bailada en
   todo el mundo.* [deh•BEE•doh ah soo FAH•mah
   een•tehr•nah•see•oh•NAHL, lah SAHL•sah ehs
   bai•LAH•dah en TOH•doh el MOON•doh] —
   (Because of its international fame, salsa is danced
   all over the world)

5. *No me gustó el final de la película; la actuación fue
   débil.* [noh meh goos•TOH el fee•NAHL deh lah
   peh•LEE•koo•lah; lah ak•too•ah•see•OHN fwee
   DEH•beel]/ — (I didn't like the ending of the movie;
   the acting was weak)

6. *Los temas universales en el cine nos permiten conectar
   a nivel global.* [lohs TEH•mahs
   oo•nee•vehr•SAH•lehs en el SEE•neh nohs
   pehr•MEE•ten koh•nek•TAR ah nee•VEL

gloh•BAHL] — (Universal themes in cinema allow us to connect on a global level)

7. *Quiero explorar la influencia generacional del dembow en la música actual.* [KYEH•ro eks•ploh•RAR lah een•floo•EHN•see•ah heh•neh•rah•see•oh•NAHL del dehm•BOW en lah MOO•see•kah ak•too•AHL] — (I want to explore the generational influence of dembow in today's music)

8. *Las ofrendas del Día de los Muertos incluyen cempasúchil para guiar a los espíritus.* [lahs oh•FREN•dahs del DEE•ah deh lohs MWER•tos een•KLOO•yen sem•pah•SOO•cheel PAH•rah gee•AR ah lohs es•PEE•ree•toos] – (The Day of the Dead offerings include marigolds to guide the spirits)

9. *Vamos al desfile juntos para celebrar con toda la comunidad.* [VAH•mos al dehs•FEE•leh HOON•tos PAH•rah seh•leh•BRAHR kon TOH•dah lah ko•moo•nee•DAHD — (Let's go to the parade together to celebrate with the entire community)

10. *La salsa tiene letras intrincadas que requieren habilidades lingüísticas y analíticas.* [lah SAHL•sah tee•E•neh LEH•tras een•treen•KAH•dahs keh reh•KYEH•ren ah•bee•lee•DAH•des leen•GWEES•tee•kahs ee ah•nah•LEE•tee•kahs] — (Salsa has intricate lyrics that require linguistic and analytical skills)

Chapter 2.2 Worksheet

1) Fill in the blanks with the correct Spanish terms and phrases related to the following themes: popular genres and artists, film and television for language learning, discussing preferences and critiques, and cultural themes in media. Use the terms and phrases provided below.

Terms and Phrases for Reference

- Reggaeton
- Shakira
- Telenovelas
- La Casa de Papel
- Películas de suspenso
- Emocionante
- Las tradiciones familiares
- Lucha contra la adversidad

Popular Genres and Artists

1. I enjoy listening to _____ music, which is a popular genre in Spanish-speaking countries.

2. One of my favorite artists is _____, who is known for their vibrant and culturally rich performances.

Film and Television for Language Learning

3. Watching _____ is a great way to improve language skills and understand cultural nuances.

4. The show _____ has received critical acclaim for its portrayal of historical events.

Discussing Preferences and Critiques

5. I prefer _____ because the storyline is more engaging.

6. The film was _____, but I found the ending to be predictable.

Cultural Themes in Media

7. The documentary highlights _____, which is a significant aspect of the culture.

8. The character's journey in the film reflects the

_____, which is a central theme in many stories from the region.

2) **Dialogue:** Ana and Carlos, discussing their favorite movies and music in Spanish.

– **Ana:** *Hola, Carlos. ¿Viste una película buena?*
[O•la, KAR•los. VEES•te OO•na peh•LEE•ku•la BWE•na?]
(Hello, Carlos. Did you see a good movie?)

– **Carlos:** *Hola, Ana. Sí, vi "La Lucha". Es sobre la identidad.*
[O•la, A•na. SEE, vi "la LOO•cha". Es SO•bre la ee•den•tee•DAHD.]
(Hello, Ana. Yes, I saw "The Struggle". It's about identity.)

– **Ana:** *¿Te gustó la actuación?*
[te goos•TO la ak•too•a•SYON?]
(Did you like the acting?)

– **Carlos:** *Sí, fue muy buena.*
[SEE, fwe MOO•ee BWE•na.]
(Yes, it was very good.)

– **Ana:** *Voy a verla. ¿Y la música? ¿Algún favorito?*
[boy ah BER•la. ee la MOO•see•kah? al•GOON
FA•vo•ree•to?]
(I will watch it. And the music? Any favorites?)

– **Carlos:** *Me gusta Rosa Lin. Sus canciones son divertidas.*
[me GOOS•ta RO•sa Lin. sus kan•see•O•nes son
dee•ber•TEE•das.]
(I like Rosa Lin. Her songs are fun.)

– **Ana:** *¡Qué bien! La música es importante.*
[KEH by•EN! La MOO•see•kah es EEM•por•tan•te.]
(That's good! Music is important.)

– **Carlos:** *¿Y a ti? ¿Qué te gusta?*
[ee a TEE? KEH te GOOS•ta?]
(And you? What do you like?)

– **Ana:** *Me gusta reír. Me gustan las comedias.*
[me GOOS-ta reh•EER. Me GOOS•tan las
ko•MEH•dee•as.]
(I like to laugh. I like comedies.)

– **Carlos:** *Muy bien. Puedo sugerir películas.*
[MOO•ee byEN. PWE•do soo•he•REER peh•LEE•ku•las.]
(Very good. I can suggest movies.)

2.3 Food Culture: Understanding Regional Cuisines

Every Hispanic country has a unique cuisine with a great variety of flavors, textures and traditions. Each region serves dishes that tell the story of its historical contexts, the geographical location where it originated and cultural fusions that happened afterwards.

Regional Specialties and Dishes

From the smoky allure of Mexican *chipotle* to the tangy zest of Peruvian *ceviche*, every dish has a regional identity. In Argentina, the *asado* stands as a testament to the country's deep-rooted love for beef, cooked over an open flame to perfection. Conversely, the Caribbean offers lighter fare, with seafood playing a starring role through dishes like *"arroz con coco"* (coconut rice) and *"pescado frito"* (fried fish).

Crossing into Spain, one encounters a culinary landscape marked by *"tapas,"* small dishes that range from *"patatas bravas"* (spicy potatoes) to *"gambas al ajillo"* (garlic shrimp), designed to encourage sharing and socializing. Meanwhile, in Central America, the humble *"pupusa,"* a stuffed corn tortilla, showcases the simplicity and richness of Salvadoran cuisine, highlighting how staple ingredients can create comforting yet complex flavors.

KEYWORDS/PHRASES AND HOW TO PRONOUNCE THEM:

1. *Chipotle* [chee•POH•tleh] — A smoked, dried jalapeño pepper used in Mexican cuisine
2. *Ceviche* [seh•VEE•cheh] — A seafood dish marinated in citrus juices, popular in Peru and other Latin American countries
3. *Asado* [ah•SAH•doh] — A barbecue or grill, particularly a grilled beef dish in Argentina
4. *Arroz con coco* [ah•RROZ con KOH•koh] — Coconut rice is a typical dish in Caribbean cuisine
5. *Pescado frito* [pes•KAH•doh FREE•toh] — Fried fish, a dish often found in tropical coastal regions
6. *Tapas* [tAh•pas] — Small dishes or appetizers, typically served in Spanish bars
7. *Patatas bravas* [pa•TAH•tas BRAH•vas] — A dish of fried potatoes served with a spicy tomato sauce, which is standard in Spain
8. *Gambas al ajillo* [GAHM•bahs al ah•HEE•yoh] — Garlic shrimp, a popular Spanish tapa
9. *Pupusa* [poo•POO•sah] — A traditional Salvadoran dish consisting of a thick corn tortilla stuffed with various fillings
10. *Sabor tropical* [sah•BOR tro•pee•KAL] — Tropical flavor

Cooking Language

Grasping the language of cooking will make you able to participate in the making and then tasting of food. Some of the key terms would be *"freír"* (to fry), *"asar"* (to roast), *"hervir"* (to boil), and *"marinar"* (to marinate). Ingredients, too, form a crucial part of this vocabulary, from *"carnes"* (meats) and *"verduras"* (vegetables) to *"especias"* (spices), each word adding to your arsenal for deciphering recipes or conversing about your latest kitchen venture.

Equally important are the tools of the trade, with items like *"sartén"* (pan), *"olla"* (pot), and *"cuchillo"* (knife) instrumental in preparing countless dishes. Knowing these terms not only aids in following recipes but also in navigating markets and kitchen stores, ensuring you're well-equipped at the time of cooking.

KEYWORDS/PHRASES AND HOW TO PRONOUNCE THEM:

1. *Freír* [freh•EER] — (to fry)
2. *Asar* [ah•SAHR] — (to roast)
3. *Hervir* [ehr•VEER] — (to boil)
4. *Marinar* [mah•ree•NAHR] — (to marinate)
5. *Carnes* [KAHR•nes] — (meats)
6. *Verduras* [ver•DOO•rahs] — (vegetables)
7. *Especias* [es•PEH•syahs] — (spices)
8. *Sartén* [sahr•TEHN] — (pan)
9. *Olla* [O•yah] — (pot)
10. *Cuchillo* [koo•CHEE•yoh] — (knife)

Dining Traditions and Meal Times

Understanding the rhythm of meal times offers insight into the social fabric of a society. Everywhere in the world food acts as a binder, bringing together family and friends. In Hispanic cultures, lunch, *"el almuerzo,"* takes center stage as the day's main meal, often extending over several hours and sometimes followed by *"la siesta,"* a brief rest to digest and recharge.

Dinner, "la cena," on the other hand, unfolds later in the evening, sometimes not until after 9 PM, as a day's end gathering. This late dining hour speaks to a lifestyle that values leisure and community, with nights stretching into social interaction.

In homes and restaurants alike, you'll often have *"sobremesas,"* the time spent lingering at the table after a meal has ended to converse with the people who just shared a meal with you.

KEYWORDS/PHRASES AND HOW TO PRONOUNCE THEM:

1. *El almuerzo* [el ahl•MWER•zo] — (lunch)
2. *La siesta* [lah see•ES•tah] — (nap)
3. *La cena* [lah SEH•nah] — (dinner)
4. *Sobremesa* [soh•breh•ME•sah] — (time spent after eating)
5. *Comida* [ko•MEE•dah] — (food)
6. *Compartir* [kohm•par•TEER] — (to share)
7. *Familia* [fah•MEE•lee•ah] — (family)

8. *Amigos* [ah•MEE•gohs] — (friends)
9. *Conversación* [kohn•ver•sah•see•OHN] — (conversation)
10. *Noche* [NOH•cheh] — (night)

Tasting and Describing Food

Describing what you're tasting expands the culinary experience, transforming each bite into an exploration of culture and geography. Vocabulary for tastes and textures, such as *"dulce"* (sweet), *"salado"* (salty), *"ácido"* (sour), *"picante"* (spicy), *"crujiente"* (crunchy), and *"suave"* (smooth), allows you to articulate the complexities of each dish, sharing your culinary journey with others.

Describing food could evoke emotions and memories. A simple "tamal" may be described as *"reconfortante"* (comforting), reminding one of family gatherings and festive celebrations. Similarly, a meal's appearance, *"la apariencia,"* from its colors to its presentation, contributes to the overall dining experience, turning each meal into a feast for the senses.

Through the lens of food culture, you're invited to savor not just the flavors but also the stories and traditions of each of these regions. Each ingredient carries a history, a pinch of geography, and a dash of soul, adding a new lawyer to your language journey.

KEYWORDS/PHRASES AND HOW TO PRONOUNCE THEM:

1. *Dulce* [DOOL•seh] — (sweet)
2. *Salado* [sah•LAH•doh] — (salty)
3. *Ácido* [AH•see•doh] — (sour)
4. *Picante* [pee•KAHN•teh] — (spicy)
5. *Crujiente* [kroo•hee•EN•teh] — (crunchy)
6. *Suave* [SWAH•veh] — (smooth)
7. *Tamal* [tah•MAHL] — (tamale)
8. *Reconfortante* [re•kohn•for•TAHN•teh] — (comforting)
9. *La apariencia* [lah ah•pah•ree•EN•see•ah] — (the appearance)
10. *Sabor* [sah•BOR] — (flavor)

Chapter 2.3 Common Spanish Phrases

1. *El ceviche tiene un sabor ácido y fresco.* [el seh•VEE•cheh tee•E•neh oon sah•BOHR AH•see•doh ee FRES•koh] — (Ceviche has a fresh and sour flavor.)
2. *Vamos a asar carne para el asado este fin de semana.* [VAH•mos ah ah•SAHR KAHR•neh PAH•rah el ah•SAH•doh ES•teh feen deh seh•MAH•nah] — (We're going to roast meat for the barbecue this weekend.)
3. *Me gusta usar chipotle en las salsas para darles un sabor ahumado.* [meh GOOS•tah oo•SAHR chee•POH•tleh en las SAHL•sahs PAH•rah DAR•les oon sah•BOHR ah•oo•MAH•doh] — (I

like to use chipotle in sauces to give them a smoky flavor.)

4. *Las pupusas se pueden rellenar con carne o verduras.* [lahs poo•POO•sahs seh PWEH•den reh•ye•NAHR kon KAHR•ne oh ver•DOO•rahs] — (Pupusas can be filled with meat or vegetables.)

5. *Para la cena, prepararemos pescado frito con arroz con coco.* [PAH•rah lah SEH•nah, preh•pah•rah•REH•mos pes•KAH•doh FREE•toh kon ah•RROZ kon KOH•koh] — (For dinner, we will prepare fried fish with coconut rice.)

6. *En España, es común comer tapas y patatas bravas con amigos.* [en es•PAH•nyah, es ko•MOON ko•MER TAH•pahs ee pa•TAH•tas BRAH•vas kon ah•MEE•gohs] — (In Spain, eating tapas and patatas bravas with friends is common.)

7. *Marinaremos las gambas al ajillo antes de freírlas.* [mah•ree•nah•REH•mos las GAHM•bahs al ah•HEE•yoh AHN•tes deh fray•EER•lahs] — (We will marinate the garlic shrimp before frying them.)

8. *La sobremesa es el mejor momento para conversar en familia.* [lah soh•breh•ME•sah es el meh•HOR mo•MEN•toh PAH•rah lah kohn•ver•sah•see•OHN en fah•MEE•lee•ah] — (The time spent after eating is the best moment for family conversation.)

9. *El arroz con coco añade un sabor tropical a cualquier cena.* [el ah•RROZ kon KOH•koh ah•NYAH•deh oon sah•BOHR troh•pee•KAL ah kwahl•KYEHR SEH•nah] — (Coconut rice adds a tropical flavor to any dinner.)

10. *Después de comer, una siesta siempre es reconfortante.*
[dehs•poo•EHS deh ko•MER, OO•nah see•ES•tah
see•EM•preh es ree•kohn•for•TAHN•teh] —
(After eating, a nap is always comforting.)

Chapter 2.3 Worksheet

1) Complete the sentences with the correct Spanish terms and phrases related to regional specialties and dishes, cooking language, dining traditions and meal times, and tasting and describing food. Use the terms from the list provided.

- *Paella:* A traditional Spanish rice dish from Valencia.
- *Tapas:* Small Spanish savory dishes, typically served with drinks at a bar.
- *Sobremesa:* The time spent after lunch or dinner talking to the people you shared the meal with.
- *Dulce:* Sweet.
- *Salado:* Salty.
- *Picante:* Spicy.
- *Crujiente:* Crunchy.
- *Suave:* Smooth.
- *Cena:* Dinner.
- *Almuerzo:* Lunch.

Sentences:

The _____ is known for being a hearty dish that originated in the south of Spain.

When you go to a bar in Spain, it's common to order _____ to share with your friends.

After a big meal, many Spaniards enjoy _____, which can last for hours.

If you prefer _____ desserts, you might like turrón or flan.

For those who like _____ food, 'gambas al ajillo' is a popular choice.

Potato chips are _____, while 'pan' is usually _____ .

The texture of 'churros' can be described as _____, especially when fresh.

A 'batido' is typically _____, perfect for a hot day.

In Spain, the main meal of the day is the _____, typically eaten in the afternoon.

_____ is the last meal of the day and is usually lighter than lunch.

2) Dialogue: Juan and María discuss dinner plans.

Juan: *Hola María, ¿quieres cocinar paella?*
[O•lah mah•REE•ah, KYEH•res ko•see•NAR pa•EH•ya?]
(Hello Maria, do you want to cook paella?)

Maria: *Sí, una paella está bien.*
[SEE, pa•EH•ya es BWE•nah]
(Yes, paella is good.)

Juan: *Es dulce y salado.*
[es DOOL•seh ee sah•LAH•doh]
(It is sweet and salty.)

Maria: *Y también ácido.*
[ee tam•BYEN AH•see•doh]
(And also sour.)

Juan: *¿Y postre?*
[ee POHS•treh?]
(And dessert?)

Maria: *Unos churros estarían bien.*
[OO•nos CHOO•rrohs sohn BWE•nos]
(Churros are good.)

Juan: *Con azúcar.*
[kon ah•SOO•kar]
(With sugar.)

Maria: *Sí, una cena española.*
[see, OO•nah SEH•nah ehs•pahn•YO•lah]
(Yes, a Spanish dinner.)

2.4 Sports and Leisure: Talking About Soccer, Baseball, and More

Sports are an important part of the idiosyncrasy of Hispanic countries as they bring people together and ignite passions across generations. Whether it's the electrifying atmosphere of a soccer stadium or the nostalgic charm of a baseball game, sports offer a unique lens through which we can experience and connect with different cultures. So, lace up your sneakers, and let's step into the world of sports and leisure in Spanish.

Key Sports Vocabulary

The realm of sports is rich with specialized vocabulary, providing the perfect playground for language learners to expand their lexicon. Here are some key sports terms:

- *Partido:* Match/Game.
- *Equipo:* Team.
- *Jugador:* Player.
- *Gol* (Soccer): Goal.
- *Carrera* (Baseball): Run.
- *Árbitro:* Referee/Umpire.
- *Estadio:* Stadium.

Familiarizing yourself with these terms enables you to follow the action more closely and engages you in discussions, allowing you to share your opinions and experiences.

Famous Athletes and Teams

Spanish-speaking countries have given the world some of its most iconic athletes and teams, figures who inspire admiration from the public. Here's some of them:

- Soccer legends like **Diego Maradona** and **Lionel Messi** from Argentina, or **Hugo Sánchez** from Mexico, have left indelible marks on the sport, their names synonymous with excellence and passion.
- In baseball, players like **Roberto Clemente** from Puerto Rico and **Pedro Martínez** from the Dominican Republic have become international symbols of talent and perseverance.
- Teams like **Real Madrid** and **FC Barcelona** in soccer or Los Tigres del Licey in baseball embody the spirit of competition, unity, and pride that sports can foster within a community.

Engaging in conversations about sports figures and teams offers a gateway into the heart of fandom. It allows you to partake in debates, share admiration, and understand the local and international sports scene more deeply.

KEYWORDS/PHRASES AND HOW TO PRONOUNCE THEM:

1. *Leyendas del fútbol* [leh•YEN•das del FOOT•bol] — (Soccer legends)
2. *Diego Maradona* [DJE•go ma•ra•DO•na] — Diego

Maradona was an Argentine soccer player widely regarded as one of the greatest in the sport.

3. *Lionel Messi* [lio•NEL ME•si] — Lionel Messi is an Argentine professional soccer player known for his incredible dribbling skills and scoring ability.

4. *Hugo Sánchez* [OO•go SAN•chez] — Hugo Sánchez is a former Mexican soccer player who is celebrated for his successful career, especially in Spanish clubs.

5. *Roberto Clemente* [ro•BER•to kle•MEN•te[— Roberto Clemente was a Puerto Rican professional baseball player who was both a Hall of Famer and a humanitarian.

6. *Pedro Martínez* [PE•dro mar•TEE•nez] — Pedro Martínez is a Dominican former professional baseball pitcher known for his time in Major League Baseball with a dominant career.

7. *Real Madrid* [re•Al ma•DREED] — Real Madrid is a professional soccer club based in Madrid, Spain, known for its rich history and numerous titles.

8. *FC Barcelona* [efe se bar•se•LO•na] — FC Barcelona is one of the world's most popular and successful soccer clubs, and it is based in Barcelona, Spain.

9. *Los Tigres del Licey* [los TEE•gres del li•SEI] — Los Tigres del Licey is a professional baseball team in the Dominican Republic, one of the oldest and most successful in the Caribbean.

10. *Espíritu de competencia* [es•pi•ri•TOO de kom•pe•TEN•sja] — (Spirit of competition | Refers to the passionate and competitive nature that drives athletes and teams to excel.)

Discussing Rules and Gameplay

Understanding and discussing the rules and gameplay of different sports adds depth to your engagement with sports events and expands your lexicon significantly. Whether it's the offside rule in soccer, *"el fuera de juego,"* that can spark endless debates, or the intricate scoring system in tennis, mastering technical aspects brings you closer to the sport. Here's how you might delve into these discussions:

- Inquire about specific rules during a game watching session: *"¿Me puedes explicar por qué eso fue un fuera de juego?"*
- Share insights on strategy and gameplay: *"Creo que deberían concentrarse más en la defensa para ganar el próximo partido."*

These dialogues refine your understanding of the sport and strengthen connections with fellow fans as you share knowledge, predictions, and post-game analysis.

KEYWORDS/PHRASES AND HOW TO PRONOUNCE THEM:

1. *Reglas* [REH•glahs] — (Rules)
2. *Juego* [HWEH•go] — (Gameplay)
3. *Fuera de juego* [FWEH•rah deh HWE•go] — (Offside)
4. *Entusiasta informado* [en•too•see•AHS•tah een•for•MAH•doh] — (Informed enthusiast)

5. *Debates sin fin* [deh•BAH•tes seen feen] — (Endless debates)
6. *Sistema de puntuación* [sees•TEH•mah deh poon•too•ah•see•OHN] — (Scoring system)
7. *¿Me puedes explicar...?* [me PWEH•des eks•plee•CAR] — (Can you explain to me...?)
8. *¿Por qué eso fue...?* [por KEH EH•soh FWE] — (Why that was)
9. *Concentrarse en la defensa* [kon•sen•TRAR•seh en lah de•FEN•sah] — (Focus on defense)
10. *Ganar el próximo partido* [ga•NAR el PROKS•ee•mo par•TEE•doh] — (Win the next match)

Cultural Importance of Sports

Sports do more than entertain; they knit the fabric of communities, embody national identities, and celebrate collective achievements. The cultural significance of sports in Hispanic societies is profound, offering insights into values, historical struggles and communal triumphs:

- **Soccer,** in many of these countries, is not just a game; it's a reflection of life's drama, a source of communal pride, and a force for social unity.
- **Baseball**, especially in the Caribbean, tells stories of colonial resistance, economic challenges, and international success, symbolizing hope and resilience.
- Events like the **Olympic Games**, where athletes compete under their national flags, become moments of collective pride and reflection,

showcasing the global stage where cultural
narratives and national identities converge.

Through sports, communities celebrate victories, lament defeats, and pass down traditions. Major sporting events turn into national holidays, streets empty during crucial matches, and generations bond over tales of games past. This shared passion offers a powerful avenue for cultural immersion, where language is the bond that unites fans across borders.

In this exploration of sports and leisure, we've seen how the universal language of sports can enrich your Spanish vocabulary, connect you to iconic figures and teams, deepen your understanding of rules and game-play, and immerse you in the cultural significance of athletic pursuits. As you navigate these conversations and experiences, you'll find that sports offer entertainment and a window into the soul of societies where every match, every cheer and every tear tells a story of community, identity, and the undying human spirit for triumph.

KEYWORDS/PHRASES AND HOW TO PRONOUNCE THEM:

1. *Cultura* [kool•TOO•ra] — (Culture)
2. *Identidad nacional* [i•den•tee•DAD na•sio•NAL] — (National identity)
3. *Logros colectivos* [LO•gros ko•lek•TEE•vos] — (Collective achievements)
4. *Fútbol* [FUT•bol] — (Soccer)

5. *Orgullo comunitario* [or•gGU•llo ko•mu•ni•TA•rio] — (Communal pride)
6. *Béisbol* [BEIS•bol] — (Baseball)
7. *Resistencia colonial* [re•sis•TEN•sia ko•lo•NJAL] — (Colonial resistance)
8. *Esperanza y resiliencia* [es•pe•RAN•za i re•si•lee•EN•sia] — (Hope and resilience)
9. *Juegos Olímpicos* [HWE•gos o•LEEM•pi•kos] — (Olympic Games)
10. *Herencia cultural* [e•REN•sia kul•tu•RAL] — (Cultural heritage)
11. *Pasión compartida* [pa•SION kom•par•TEE•da] — (Shared passion)
12. *Triunfos y derrotas* [tri•UN•fos i de•RRO•tas] — (Victories and defeats)
13. *Figuras icónicas* [fi•GU•ras i•KO•ni•cas] — (Iconic figures)
14. *Inmersión cultural* [in•mer•SION kul•tu•RAL] — (Cultural immersion)
15. *Espíritu humano* [es•PEE•ritu u•MA•no] — (Human spirit)

Chapter 2.4 Common Spanish Phrases

1. *Diego Maradona es una de las leyendas del fútbol más recordadas.* [DJE•go ma•ra•DO•na es OO•nah de las leh•YEN•das del FUT•bol mas re•kor•DA•das] — (Diego Maradona is one of the most remembered soccer legends.)
2. *Lionel Messi ha ganado fama internacional por su habilidad en el campo.* [lio•NEL ME•si ah ga•NA•do

FAH•mah EEN•tehr•nah•see•oh•nahl por soo
ah•bee•lee•dAhd en el kAhm•po] — Lionel Messi
has gained international fame for his skill on the
field.

3. *Real Madrid y FC Barcelona son rivales históricos en el
   fútbol.* [re•AL ma•DREED ee efesSE bar•se•LO•na
   son ree•VAH•les ees•TOH•ree•kos en el FUT•bol]
   — Real Madrid and FC Barcelona are historic rivals
   in soccer.

4. *Los Tigres del Licey muestran el espíritu de
   competencia del béisbol caribeño.* [los tee•GRES del
   li•SEI MWES•tran el es•PEE•ritu de
   kom•pe•TEN•sja del BEIS•bol ka•ree•BE•ño] —
   Los Tigres del Licey show the spirit of competition
   of Caribbean baseball.

5. *La pasión por el fútbol es parte de nuestra identidad
   nacional.* [lah pah•SION por el FUT•bol es pAr•te
   de NUES•tra i•den•ti•DAD na•sio•NAL] —
   Passion for soccer is part of our national identity.

6. *Pedro Martínez inspira a jóvenes con sus logros
   colectivos en el béisbol.* [PE•dro mar•TEE•nez
   eens•PEE•rah ah HO•ve•nes kon soos LO•gros
   ko•lek•TEE•vos en el BEIS•bol] — Pedro Martínez
   inspires young people with his collective
   achievements in baseball.

7. *El fútbol une a las personas y fomenta el orgullo
   comunitario.* [el FUT•bol OO•ne a las per•SO•nas
   ee fo•MEN•ta el or•GU•yo ko•mu•ni•TA•rio] —
   Soccer unites people and fosters communal pride.

8. *¿Me puedes explicar las reglas del fuera de juego en el
   fútbol?* [me PWE•des eks•plee•CAR las REH•glahs

del FWEH•rah deh HWEgo en el FUT•bol?] —
Can you explain the offside rules in soccer to me?

9. ***La victoria de Hugo Sánchez con el Real Madrid es un triunfo para México.*** [la vik•TO•ria de U•go SAN•chez kon el re•AL ma•DREED es oon tri•UN•fo para ME•hi•ko] — Hugo Sánchez's victory with Real Madrid is a triumph for Mexico.

10. ***Los Juegos Olímpicos son una muestra del espíritu humano y la esperanza.*** [los HWE•gos o•LEEM•pi•kos son oona MWES•tra del es•PEE•ritu u•MA•no ee la es•pe•RAN•za] — The Olympic Games are a showcase of the human spirit and hope.

Chapter 2.4 Worksheet

1) Fill in the blanks using the words provided in the list below:

List of Words

- Orgullo comunal
- Esperanza y resiliencia
- Juegos Olímpicos
- Orgullo nacional
- Inmersión cultural
- Fuera de juego
- La defensa
- Atletas famosos
- Equipos
- Partido
- Derrota

- Comunidad

Cultural Importance of Sports

Soccer is not just a game; it's a reflection of life's drama and a source of (communal pride)

_____

Baseball in the Caribbean tells stories of colonial resistance and symbolizes (hope and resilience)

_____

The _____ (Olympic Games) become moments of collective _____ (national pride) and reflection.

Sports serve as a powerful avenue for (cultural immersion)

_____

Discussing Rules and Gameplay

The offside rule in soccer, known as _____ (el fuera de juego), can spark endless debates.

During a game, one might ask, "_¿Me puedes explicar por qué eso fue un_ (fuera de juego)?"

_____

It's often said that teams should concentrate on (defense) _____to win the game.

Famous Athletes and Teams

(Famous athletes) _____ and (teams) _____ often become national heroes.

Cheering for (teams) _____ can unite people across different backgrounds.

Key Sports Vocabulary

Every (match) _____ tells a story of community and spirit.

Victories and (defeats) _____ are shared by the entire (community) _____.

2) Dialogue: Ana and Luis discuss *fútbol.* Try and pronounce each word with a Spanish accent.

Ana: *Hola, Luis. ¿Viste el fútbol ayer?*
[O•lah, LOO•eess. VEES•teh el FUT•bol a•YEHR?]
(Hello, Luis. Did you watch the soccer match yesterday?)

Luis: *¡Sí, Ana! Fue emocionante. Me gusta el fútbol.*
[SEE, AH•nah! fwe eh•mo•see•o•NAHN•teh. meh goose•TAH el FUT•bol.]
(Yes, Ana! It was exciting. I like soccer.)

Ana: *¿Puedes explicar la regla del fuera de juego? No entiendo.*
[PWEH•des eks•plee•CAR la REH•glah del FWEH•-rah deh HWEH•goh? no en•tee•EN•doh.]
(Can you explain the offside rule? I don't understand.)

Luis: *Claro. Si un jugador recibe el balón y solo hay un jugador contrario entre él y la meta, está en fuera de juego.*
[CLAH•roh. see oon hoo•gah•DOR reh•SEE•beh el bah•LON ee SOH•loh eye oon hoo•gah•DOR con•TRAH•ree•oh EN•treh ehl ee la MEH•tah, es•TAH en FWEH•rah deh HWEH•goh.]
(Sure. If a player gets the ball and there is only one opposing player between him and the goal, he is offside.)

Ana: *Entiendo. ¿Qué piensas de Messi o Ronaldo?*
[en•tee•EN•doh. KEH pee•EN•sahs deh Messi oh Ronaldo?]
(I understand. What do you think of Messi or Ronaldo?)

Luis: *Son muy buenos. Trabajan mucho y juegan bien.*
[son MOO•ee BWEH•nos. trah•BAH•han MOO•choh ee HWEH•gahn bee•EN.]
(They are very good. They work hard and play well.)

Ana: *Sí, son como héroes. Especialmente en los juegos olímpicos.*
[SEE, son KOH•moh EH•roh•es. es•peh•see•AL•men•teh en los HWEH•gos oh•LEEM•pee•kos.]
(Yes, they are like heroes. Especially in the Olympic Games.)

Luis: *Sí. Y hablar de deportes nos ayuda a aprender.*
[SEE. ee ah•BLAR deh deh•POR•tes nos ah•YOO•dah ah ah•PREHN•der.]
(Yes. And talking about sports helps us learn.)

Ana: ¡Interesante! Hablemos más de deportes en español.
[een•teh•reh•SAHN•teh! ah•BLEH•mos MAHS deh
deh•POR•tes en es•pah•NYOL.]
(Interesting! Let's talk more about sports in Spanish.)

2.5 Historical and Cultural Landmarks: Exploring the Spanish-Speaking World

When we gaze at the historical and cultural landmarks that
dot the landscapes of Spanish-speaking countries, we find
ourselves stepping into a world where every stone, every
mural, and every ancient ruin tells a tale. These stories,
etched into the very fabric of these nations, offer a glimpse
into the past that shaped the cultures we see today.

Famous Landmarks and Their Stories

From the majestic ruins of Machu Picchu in Peru, a testament to the ingenuity of the Inca civilization, to the
grandeur of Spain's Alhambra, a palace that whispers tales
of the Nasrid dynasty, these landmarks serve as bridges to
bygone eras. Each visit to places like Mexico's Chichen Itzá
or Argentina's Perito Moreno Glacier isn't just a tick on a
travel bucket list; it's an encounter with history, a lesson in
the resilience and artistry of human civilizations.

- **Machu Picchu:** Often shrouded in mist and
  mystery, this ancient city offers insight into Inca
  architecture and their harmonious relationship
  with nature.

- **Alhambra:** This fortress-palace complex in Granada showcases Islamic art and architecture, reflecting the cultural fusion that characterizes much of Spain's history.

These landmarks are not just attractions but narratives set in stone, inviting travelers to listen, learn, and connect with the past.

KEYWORDS/PHRASES AND HOW TO PRONOUNCE THEM:

1. Ruinas [RROO•een•as] — (Ruins)

- Example: "Las ruinas de Machu Picchu son impresionantes." — (The ruins of Machu Picchu are impressive.)

2. Ingenio [een•HEN•ee•oh] — (Ingenuity)

- Example: "El ingenio de la civilización Inca es evidente en Machu Picchu." — (The ingenuity of the Inca civilization is evident in Machu Picchu.)

3. Palacio [pah•LAH•see•oh] — (Palace)

- Example: "La Alhambra era un palacio de la dinastía Nasrid." — (The Alhambra was a palace of the Nasrid dynasty.)

4. Grandiosidad [gran•dee•oh•see•DAHD] — (Grandeur)

- Example: "La grandiosidad de la Alhambra es conocida mundialmente." — (The grandeur of the Alhambra is known worldwide.)

5. Puente [PWEN•teh] — (Bridge)

- Example: "Estos lugares sirven como un puente a épocas pasadas." — (These places serve as a bridge to bygone eras.)

6. Encuentro [en•KWEN•troh] — [Encounter]

- Example: "Cada visita es un encuentro con la historia." — (Each visit is an encounter with history.)

7. Resiliencia [reh•see•lee•EN•see•ah] — Resilience

- Example: "Estas visitas son una lección de resiliencia humana." — (These visits are a lesson in human resilience.)

8. Arte [AR•teh] — (Art)

- Example: "La Alhambra es un escaparate del arte islámico." — (The Alhambra is a showcase of Islamic art.)

9. Arquitectura [ar•kee•tek•TOO•rah] — (Architecture)

- Example: "Machu Picchu ofrece una visión de la arquitectura Inca." — (Machu Picchu offers insight into Inca architecture.)

10. Naturaleza [nah•too•rah•LEH•thah] — (Nature)

- Example: "Machu Picchu muestra la relación armónica con la naturaleza." — (Machu Picchu shows the harmonious relationship with nature.)

Geography and Travel Vocabulary

To truly engage with these stories, a traveler's vocabulary needs to extend beyond the basic *"mapa"* (map) and *"guía"* (guide). Words like *"patrimonio"* (heritage) and *"ruinas"* (ruins) become keys to unlocking more profound dialogues about these sites. Making questions such as *"¿Cuál es la historia detrás de...?"* (What is the story behind...?) open doors to understanding the significance of each landmark.

- *Paisaje* (Landscape): Describing the surrounding scenery enhances the narrative of each landmark.
- *Excursión guiada* (Guided tour): Opting for these tours often provides enriched insights into the historical context.

Armed with this vocabulary, conversations transition from mere observations to meaningful exchanges about each site's historical and cultural essence.

KEYWORDS/PHRASES AND HOW TO PRONOUNCE THEM:

1. Mapa [MAH•pah] — (Map)

- Example: "Necesitamos un mapa para explorar la ciudad." — (We need a map to explore the city.)

2. Guía [GHEE•ah] — (Guide)

- Example: "El guía nos mostrará los lugares históricos." — (The guide will show us the historical places.)

3. Patrimonio [pa•tree•MOH•nee•oh] — (Heritage)

- Example: "Este sitio es patrimonio mundial." — (This site is a world heritage.)

4. Ruinas [rroo•EEN•as] — (Ruins)

- Example: "Las ruinas revelan mucho sobre el pasado." — (The ruins reveal a lot about the past.)

5. Historia [ees•TO•ree•ah] — (History)

- Example: "¿Cuál es la historia detrás de este edificio?" — (What is the history behind this building?)

6. Paisaje [pah•ees•AH•heh] — (Landscape)

- Example: "El paisaje aquí es absolutamente hermoso." — (The landscape here is absolutely beautiful.)

7. Excursión guiada [eks•kur•SYOHN ghee•AH•dah] — (Guided tour)

- Example: "Vamos a tomar una excursión guiada por el parque nacional." — (We are going to take a guided tour of the national park.)

8. Significado [see•nee•fee•KAH•doh] — (Significance)

- Example: "El significado de este lugar es profundo." — (The significance of this place is profound.)

9. Diálogos [dee•AH•loh•gohs] — (Dialogues)

- Example: "Estos diálogos sobre historia son muy interesantes." — (These dialogues about history are very interesting.)

10. Observaciones [ob•ser•va•see•OH•nes] — (Observations)

- Example: "Mis observaciones del arte antiguo me han enseñado mucho." — (My observations of ancient art have taught me a lot.)

Cultural Heritage and Preservation

The efforts to preserve these landmarks go beyond maintaining bricks and mortar; they are about safeguarding a nation's soul, stories, and identity. UNESCO World Heritage sites, such as Colombia's Cartagena, are recognized for their aesthetic or historical value and role in humanity's collective memory.

- *Conservación* (Conservation): This term encompasses the myriad efforts to protect and maintain these sites for future generations.
- *Sostenibilidad* (Sustainability) is a crucial preservation aspect, ensuring that tourism and interaction with these sites do not compromise their integrity.

Learning about these efforts inspires a greater appreciation for each visit, transforming tourists into informed and respectful guardians of cultural heritage.

KEYWORDS/PHRASES AND HOW TO PRONOUNCE THEM:

1. *Conservación* [kon•ser•vah•see•ON] — (Conservation)
2. *Sostenibilidad* [sohs•teh•nee•bee•lee•DAHD] — (Sustainability)
3. *Patrimonio de la Humanidad* [pa•tree•MOH•nee•oh deh lah oo•mah•nee•DAHD] — (UNESCO World Heritage)

4. *Cartagena* [car•tah•HEH•nah] — (Cartagena)
5. *Integridad* [een•teh•gree•DAHD] — (Integrity)
6. *Identidad* [ee•den•tee•DAHD] — (Identity)
7. *Esforzarse* [es•for•ZAR•seh] — (To strive)
8. *Guardián* [gwar•dee•AHN] — (Guardian)
9. *Memoria colectiva* [meh•MOH•ree•ah koh•lehk•TEE•va] — (Collective memory)
10. *Valor estético* [vah•LOR es•TAY•tee•koh] — (Aesthetic value | The value of a place or object based on its beauty and artistic importance.)

Planning a Culturally Immersive Trip

Embarking on a journey that transcends the typical tourist experience involves immersing oneself in the destination's culture, history and people. This means stepping off the beaten path to explore *"barrios históricos"* (historic neighborhoods) or engaging with *"artesanías locales"* (local crafts) that tell the story of a place and its people.

- *Inmersión cultural* (**Cultural immersion**): To strive for experiences that allow a deeper understanding and connection with the local culture.
- *Intercambio* (**Exchange**): Engaging with locals, sharing stories, and learning from each other.

Such trips don't just create memories; they weave the traveler into the place's history, leaving an imprint on the soul far beyond the journey home.

As we close this chapter, we reflect on the landmarks and stories that beckon from Hispanic countries. These places are more than dots on a map; they are keepers of history, art and culture, inviting others to explore, learn and connect. Our exploration might begin from the comfort of our couch, but it leads us to complex and interesting cultures, each landmark a chapter in the grand narrative of human civilization. As we turn the page, we carry with us memories and a deeper understanding of the world and our place within it, ready to step into the next adventure that awaits.

KEYWORDS/PHRASES AND HOW TO PRONOUNCE THEM:

1. Barrios históricos [BAHR•ree•ohs ees•TO•ree•kohs] — (Historic neighborhoods)

- Example: "Vamos a caminar por los barrios históricos para entender la cultura de la ciudad." — (Let's walk through the historic neighborhoods to understand the city's culture.)

2. Artesanías locales [ahr•teh•sah•NEE•ahs loh•KA•les] — (Local crafts)

- Example: "Las artesanías locales reflejan la tradición del lugar." — (Local crafts reflect the tradition of the place.9

3. Inmersión cultural [een•mer•SYOHN kool•too•RAHL] — (Cultural immersion)

- Example: "Busco una inmersión cultural para conocer mejor el país." — (I'm looking for a cultural immersion to better know the country.)

4. Intercambio [een•ter•KAHM•byoh] — (Exchange)

- Example: "El intercambio con los locales es la mejor parte del viaje." — (The exchange with the locals is the best part of the trip.)

5. Cultura [kool•TOO•rah] — (Culture)

- Example: "La cultura de esta región es única y fascinante." — (The culture of this region is unique and fascinating.)

6. Historia [ees•TO•reeah] — History

- Example: "La historia de este lugar se siente en cada calle." — (The history of this place is felt in every street.)

7. Gente [HEN•teh] — People

- Example: "La gente de aquí es conocida por su hospitalidad." — (The people here are known for their hospitality.)

8. *Experiencia* [ehks•peh•ree•EN•see•ah] — (Experience)

- Example: "Esta experiencia me ha cambiado la vida." — (This experience has changed my life.)

9. *Respeto* [rehs•PEH•toh] — (Respect)

- Example: "Viajar con respeto hacia otras culturas es esencial." — (Traveling with respect towards other cultures is essential.)

10. *Recuerdos* (re•ku•ER•dos) — (Memories)

- Example: "Me llevo recuerdos inolvidables de este viaje." — (I take unforgettable memories from this trip.)

Chapter 2.5 Common Spanish Phrases

1. ***Las ruinas de Cartagena son un testimonio de su rica historia.*** [lahs RROO•een•as de car•tah•HEH•nah son oon tes•tee•MOH•nee•oh de soo REE•kah ees•TO•ree•ah] — (The ruins of Cartagena are a testimony to its rich history.)

2. ***El ingenio de los constructores se refleja en la arquitectura del palacio.*** [el een•HEN•nee•oh de los kons•truk•TOH•res se reh•FLEH•ha en la ar•kee•tek•TOO•rah del pah•LAH•see•oh] — (The ingenuity of the builders is reflected in the architecture of the palace.)

3. *La grandiosidad de Machu Picchu atrae a visitantes de todo el mundo.* [lah gran•dee•oh•see•DAHD de MAH•choo PEE•choo ah•TRAH•eh ah vee•SEE•tahn•tes de TOH•doh el MOON•doh] — (The grandeur of Machu Picchu attracts visitors from all over the world.)

4. *Caminar por el puente es como un encuentro directo con la naturaleza.* [kah•mee•NAR por el PWEN•teh es KOH•moh oon en•KWEN•troh dee•REK•toh kohn lah nah•too•rah•LEH•thah] — (Walking over the bridge is like a direct encounter with nature.)

5. *Visitar estas ruinas es una lección de resiliencia y arte.* [vee•see•TAR ES•tahs RROO•ee•nas es oo•nah lehk•see•ON de reh•see•lee•EN•see•ah ee AR•teh] — (Visiting these ruins is a lesson in resilience and art.)

6. *Necesitamos un guía para explorar el patrimonio histórico de la ciudad.* [neh•seh•see•TAH•mohs oon GHEE•ah PAH•rah eks•ploh•RAR el pa•tree•MOH•nee•oh ees•TO•ree•koh de lah see•oo•DAHD] — (We need a guide to explore the city's historical heritage.)

7. *La excursión guiada al parque nacional nos mostrará su importancia natural.* [lah eks•kur•SYOHN ghee•AH•dah ahl PAR•keh nah•see•oh•NAHL nohs mos•trah•RAH soo eem•por•TAHN•see•a nah•too•RAHL] — (The guided tour of the national park will show us its natural significance.)

8. *Estas observaciones sobre la arquitectura Inca demuestran su conexión con la naturaleza.* [ES•tahs ob•ser•va•see•OH•nes SOH•bre lah

ar•kee•tek•TOO•rah EEN•kah deh•MWES•tran
soo ko•nek•see•ON kohn lah
nah•too•rah•LEH•thah] — (These observations
about Inca architecture demonstrate its connection
with nature.)

9. *El arte y la arquitectura de la Alhambra son un escaparate de su cultura.* [el AR•teh ee lah ar•kee•tek•TOO•rah de lah al•HAM•brah son oon es•ka•pah•RAH•teh de soo kool•TOO•rah] — (The art and architecture of the Alhambra are a showcase of its culture.)

10. *Explorar los barrios históricos ofrece una inmersión cultural única.* [eks•ploh•RAR los BAH•rree•ohs ees•TO•ree•kohs oh•FREH•seh OO•nah een•mer•SYOHN kool•too•RAL OO•nee•kah] — (Exploring the historic neighborhoods offers a unique cultural immersion.)

Chapter 2.5 Worksheet

1) Fill in the blanks using the selected phrases and words in Spanish.

Planning a Culturally Immersive Trip

- Striving for experiences that allow for a deeper understanding and connection with the local culture is known as_____(*cultural immersion*).

- Engaging with locals, sharing stories, and learning from each other enriches the travel experience and fosters mutual respect, a process known as _____ (*exchange*).

Cultural Heritage and Preservation

- The term _____ (*conservation*) encompasses the myriad efforts to protect and maintain these sites for future generations.
- _____ (*sustainability*) is a crucial aspect of preservation, ensuring that tourism and interaction with these sites do not compromise their integrity.

Geography and Travel Vocabulary

- To truly engage with these stories, a traveler's vocabulary needs to extend beyond the basic _____ (*map*) and _____ (*guide*). Words like _____ (*heritage*) and _____ (*ruins*) become keys to unlocking more profound dialogues about these sites.
- Phrases such as "*¿Cuál es la*_____*detrás de...?*" (What is the story behind...?) can help us understand the significance of each landmark.

Famous Landmarks and Their Stories

* Every landmark has a story, often interwoven with
  the nation's history and cultural identity. The
  majestic _____ (*palace*) of Spain,
  the ancient _____(*temple*) of
  Mexico, and the iconic _____
  (*statue*) of Argentina are not merely structures; they
  are symbols of the people's resilience and creativity.

2) **Dialogue:** Read the conversation aloud and try to
pronounce the Spanish words with a Spanish accent:

Luis: *Hola Elena, ¿te gustaría ir a Machu Picchu conmigo?*
[O•lah eh•LEH•nah, teh goos•tah•REE•ah eer ah
MAH•choo PEE•choo kohn•MEE•goh?]
(Hi Elena, would you like to go to Machu Picchu with me?)

Elena: *Sí, Luis. Quiero hacer una inmersión cultural.*
[SEE, loo•EES. KYEH•roh ah•SEHR OO•nah
een•mer•SYOHN kool•too•RAHL.]
(Yes, Luis. I want to have a cultural immersion.)

Luis: *Es un buen lugar para aprender sobre el patrimonio de los
Incas.*
[ehs oon BWEHN LOO•gahr PAH•rah ah•prehn•DEHR
SOH•breh el pah•tree•MOH•nee•oh deh lohs EEN•kahs.]
(It's a good place to learn about the heritage of the Incas.)

Elena: *Debemos tomar una excursión guiada para entender su historia.*
[deh•BEH•mohs toh•MAHR OO•nah eks•kur•SYOHN gee•AH•dah PAH•rah ehn•ten•DEHR lah ees•TOH•ree•ah.]
(We should take a guided tour to understand the history.)

Luis: *También quiero ver el paisaje y la geografía del lugar.*
[tahm•BYEHN KYEH•roh vehr el pah•ee•SAH•heh ee lah heh•oh•GRAH•fee•ah del LOO•gahr.]
(I also want to see the landscape and geography of the place.)

Elena: *Sí, y podemos hablar con los guías sobre la conservación de las ruinas.*
[SEE, ee poh•DEH•mohs ah•BLAHR kohn lohs GEE•ahs SOH•breh lah kohn•ser•va•SYOHN deh lahs rroo•EE•nahs.]
(Yes, and we can talk to the guides about the conservation of the ruins.)

Luis: *Machu Picchu es más que un sitio turístico; es una experiencia única.*
[MAH•choo PEE•choo ehs mahs keh oon SEE•tee•oh too•REES•tee•koh; ehs OO•nah eks•peh•ree•EN•see•ah OO•nee•kah.]
(Machu Picchu is more than a tourist site; it's a unique experience.)

Elena: *Estoy emocionada por esta aventura.*
[es•TOY eh•moh•see•oh•NAH•dah pohr EHS•tah
ah•ven•TOO•rah.]
(I am excited about this adventure.)

THREE

Mastering Conversational Spanish

P icture this: you're at a bustling local market under the sun, surrounded by the lively chatter of vendors and shoppers. The air is filled with the scent of fresh produce and the sound of bargaining. Here, amidst the colors and sounds, lies the perfect setting for everyday conversations, which weaves the fabric of daily life in Hispanic communities. From casual greetings to discussions about weather, these interactions are the threads that connect us, offering invaluable opportunities to practice and deepen our understanding of the Spanish language and Hispanic cultures.

3.1 Everyday Conversations: Chatting with Friends and Neighbors

Initiating Small Talk

Small talk isn't just about filling silence; it's an art form that opens doors to deeper connections. Start with the basics like the weather, *"¿Qué tal el clima hoy?"* (How's the weather today?), or local events, *"¿Vas a la feria este fin de semana?"* (Are you going to the fair this weekend?). These simple inquiries show interest in the other person's life and can lead to more engaging conversations.

Situations for Small Talk include waiting in line, riding public transportation, or even a brief encounter with a neighbor.

KEYWORDS/PHRASES AND HOW TO PRONOUNCE THEM:

1. Hola [O•la] — (Hello)

2. ¿Qué tal? [KEH tal] — (How are you?)

3. El clima [el KLEE•ma] — (The weather)

4. Hoy [oy] — (Today)

5. ¿Qué tal el clima hoy? [KEH tal el KLEE•ma oy] (How's the weather today?)

6. La feria [la FEH•ria] — (The fair)

7. Este fin de semana [EHS•te fin de se•MA•na] — (This weekend)

8. *¿Vas a la feria este fin de semana?* [vas a la FEH•ria EHS•te fin de se•MA•na] — (Are you going to the fair this weekend?)

9. *Esperando* [es•pe•RAN•do] — (Waiting)

10. *El transporte público* [el trans•POR•te POO•bli•ko] — (Public transportation)

Additional Conversation Starters:

11. *¿Has visto...?* [as VEES•to] — (Have you seen...?)

- Use this to ask about recent movies, TV shows, or events.

12. *¿Qué me cuentas?* [KEH me KWEN•tas/ — (What can you tell me?)

- It is a casual way to ask for news or updates from someone's life.

13. *¿Qué planes tienes para...?* [KEH PLAH•nes TJE•nes PAH•ra?] — (What plans do you have for...?)

- Great for asking about upcoming weekend plans or holidays.

14. *El vecino* [el ve•si•no] — (The neighbor)

- It is helpful when starting conversations about neighborhood news or questions.

15. *Me gusta...* [me GOOS•ta] — (I like...)

- Share something you enjoy to find common interests.

16. ¿Y tú? [ee TOO] — (And you?)

- Perfect for turning the question back on the speaker and showing interest.

Common Colloquial Phrases

Diving into the pool of colloquialisms of the place you are in adds color to your conversations, making them more natural and relatable. Phrases like *"¿Qué onda?"* (What's up?) or *"Estoy a tope"* (I'm swamped) offer a glimpse into how locals express themselves daily.

- **Exercise:** In your next chat, try swapping out textbook phrases for these colloquial alternatives.
- **Resource List:** Keep a list of frequently heard slang and expressions, noting their meanings and contexts.

KEYWORDS/PHRASES AND HOW TO PRONOUNCE THEM:

1. *¿Qué onda?* [KEH ON•da] — (What's up?)

2. *Estoy a tope* [es•TOY a TOH•pe] — (I'm swamped)

3. *Chévere* [CHE•ve•re] — (Cool, awesome)

4. ¿Cómo vas? [KO•mo vas] — (How's it going?)

5. A full [a full] — (Full on, intensely)

6. Ni idea [ni i•deh•ah] — (No idea)

7. ¿Qué tal? [KEH tal] — (How are you?/What's up?)

8. Vale [va•le] — (Okay)

9. Guay [gway] — (Cool, awesome)

10. No pasa nada [no PAH•sa NA•da] — (No worries/It's okay)

Additional Colloquial Phrases:

11. Estoy hecho polvo [es•TOY EH•cho POL•vo] — (I'm exhausted)

- Use this to express tiredness or exhaustion more locally.

12. Tío/Tía [TEE•o/TEE•a] — (Dude/Guy/Lady)

- Commonly used among friends or peers.

13. Me mola [me MOH•la] — (I like it)

- A casual way to express liking something.

14. Qué fuerte [KEH FWER•te] — (That's intense/That's crazy)

- Used to express surprise or disbelief.

15. Estar en las nubes [es•TAR en las NOO•bes] — (To be daydreaming)

- It literally means "to be in the clouds," used when someone is not paying attention or lost in thought.

Listening for Context

Understanding isn't just about catching every word; it's about grasping the message. When words escape you, pay attention to body language, tone and situation to fill in gaps. This context can tell whether a person is joking, serious, or inviting you to a local gathering.

- **Interactive Element:** Practice with a friend or language partner, focusing on non-verbal cues.
- **Scenario:** Someone's tone and relaxed posture at a café might indicate they're in no rush, possibly opening the door for a more extended conversation.

KEYWORDS/PHRASES AND HOW TO PRONOUNCE THEM:

1. Entender [en•ten•DEHR] — (To understand)

2. Mensaje [men•SA•he] — (Message)

3. Lenguaje corporal [len•GWA•he kor•po•RAL] — (Body language)

4. Tono [TO•no] — (Tone)

5. Situación [si•twa•CION] — (Situation)

6. Broma [BRO•ma] — (Joke)

7. Serio [SEH•rio] — (Serious)

8. Invitación [in•vi•ta•CION] — (Invitation)

9. Reunión local [re•oo•NION lo•CAL] — (Local gathering)

10. Señal [se•NYAL] — (Cue)

Additional Phrases for Context Understanding:

11. ¿Estás bromeando? [es•TAS bro•MEAN•do] — (Are you joking?)

- It helps clarify if someone is making a joke.

12. Pareces serio [pa•RE•ces SEH•rio] — (You seem serious)

- A phrase to comment on someone's serious demeanor.

13. ¿Te gustaría...? [te gus•ta•REEA...?] — (Would you like...?)

- When someone is extending an invitation.

14. Sin prisa [sin PREE•sa] — (No rush)

- Indicates that there's no hurry, possibly opening up for more interaction.

15. *Hablemos más* [ha•BLEH•mos MAS] — (Let's talk more)

- Suggesting to continue the conversation, indicating interest in a more extended dialogue.

Interactive Element:

Pay close attention to non-verbal cues such as facial expressions, gestures, and posture when practicing with a friend or language partner. This practice helps in understanding the context and overall message of the conversation, even when you might not catch every word.

Scenario Tip:

In a casual setting like a café, observing someone's *"tono"* (tone) and *"postura relajada"* (relaxed posture) can give you hints about their openness to engage in conversation. If they seem relaxed and smiley, it might be an excellent opportunity to start a conversation with phrases like *"¿Puedo unirme?"* [PWE•do oo•NEER•me] (Can I join you?).

Cultural Nuances in Casual Conversation

The rhythm of conversation varies significantly across the Spanish-speaking world. In some places, interactions might be more direct, while formality and politeness reign in others. For instance, in many parts of Latin America, greeting with a light hug or cheek kiss among friends is common, a gesture that conveys warmth and acceptance.

- **Visual Element:** Keep an infographic showcasing greeting customs in various Spanish-speaking countries.
- **Why It Matters:** Adapting to these nuances shows respect and fosters a more profound sense of belonging.

Through these pillars of everyday conversation, from initiating small talk to navigating cultural nuances, you enhance your linguistic skills and ability to connect with native speakers. The beauty of language learning lies not just in mastering grammar or expanding vocabulary but in breaking down barriers, one casual chat at a time. Each interaction can transform a simple conversation into a bridge between worlds, inviting a richer, more nuanced understanding of the tapestry of Spanish-speaking cultures.

1. Ritmo [REET•mo] – (Rythm)

2. Conversación [kon•ver•tha•THEEON] (Spain) or [kon•ver•sa•SION] (Latin America) – (Conversation)

3. Directo [di•REK•to] – (Direct)

4. Formalidad [for•ma•li•DAHD] – (Formality)

5. Cortesía [kor•te•SEEA] – (Politeness)

6. Saludo [sa•LOO•do] – (Greeting)

7. Abrazo [a•BRAH•tho] (Spain) or [a•BRAH•so] (Latin America) – (Hug)

8. Beso en la mejilla [BEH•so en la me•HEE•ya] – (Cheek kiss)

9. Calidez [ka•li•DEZ] – (Warmth)

10. Aceptación [a•cep•ta•THEEON] (Spain) or [a•sep•ta•SION] (Latin America) – (Acceptance)

Additional Phrases for Cultural Understanding:

11. ¿Cómo te va? [KO•mo te VA] – (How's it going?)

- It is a friendly way to start a conversation, showing interest in the other's well-being.

12. Mucho gusto [MOO•cho GOOS•to] – (Nice to meet you)

- Expresses pleasure in meeting someone, a common phrase during introductions.

13. Disculpa [dis•KOOL•pa] – (Excuse me/Sorry)

- Used to apologize or get someone's attention politely.

14. Por favor [por fa•vor] – (Please)

15. Gracias [GRA•theeas] (Spain) or [GRA•sias] (Latin America) – (Thank You)

Why It Matters:

Adapting to the cultural nuances of conversation in Spanish-speaking countries demonstrates respect and helps form stronger connections. Whether greeting someone with a *"beso en la mejilla"* or exchanging pleasantries, understanding these subtle differences can significantly enhance your communication skills and ability to integrate into the community. The *"beso en la mejilla"* (cheek kiss) is a common greeting in many Hispanic countries, though the specifics can vary widely by region. This gesture is typically seen as a sign of warmth and friendship. Here's an overview of how the cheek kiss is practiced in different Spanish-speaking countries:

Spain

- **Number of Kisses:** Usually two, one on each cheek.
- **Who:** Common among women and between men and women; men usually greet with a handshake unless very close.

Argentina

- **Number of Kisses:** One.
- **Who:** Universal among men and women, even in more formal settings or when meeting for the first time.

Chile

- **Number of Kisses:** One, primarily on the right cheek.
- **Who:** Predominantly between women and between men and women; not as common between men unless they are family or close friends.

Mexico

- **Number of Kisses:** Kisses are not as common as handshakes, but one kiss is typical when more familiarity is present.
- **Who:** Generally between women and from men to women; men tend to prefer handshakes.

Colombia

- **Number of Kisses:** One.
- **Who:** Similar to Argentina, though slightly less common in professional environments.

Peru

- **Number of Kisses:** One is common, particularly in urban areas like Lima.
- **Who:** More frequent among women or between men and women; less common between two men.

Venezuela

- **Number of Kisses:** One.
- **Who:** It is widely accepted between women and between men and women; it is only common between two men if they are very close.

Cuba

- **Number of Kisses:** One.
- **Who:** Common in social settings among women and between men and women; not typical between men.

Uruguay

- **Number of Kisses:** One.
- **Who:** Like Argentina, the cheek kiss is widespread and used in most social contexts.

Central America

- Practices can vary significantly, but the cheek kiss is generally less common than in South America. Handshakes and verbal greetings are more typical, with cheek kisses reserved for closer relationships or specific social circles.

Chapter 3.1 Common Spanish Phrases

1. *¿Qué tal el clima hoy?* [KEH tal el KLEE•ma oy] — How's the weather today?
2. *¿Vas a la feria este fin de semana?* [vas a la FEH•ria ES•te fin de se•MAH•na] — Are you going to the fair this weekend?
3. *Estoy esperando el transporte público.* [es•TOI es•pe•RAN•do el trans•POR•te POO•bli•ko] — I'm waiting for public transportation.

4. *¿Qué me cuentas de nuevo?* [KEH me KWEN•tas de NWE•vo] — What can you tell me that's new?

5. *¿Qué planes tienes para el próximo fin de semana?* [KEH PLAH•nes TJE•nes PAH•ra el PROK•si•mo fin de SEH•ma•na] — What plans do you have for next weekend?

6. *Me gusta pasar tiempo con los vecinos.* [me GOOS•ta PAH•sar TJEM•po kon los ve•SEE•nos] — I like spending time with the neighbors.

7. *¿Y tú, qué onda?* [i TOO, KEH ON•da] — And you, what's up?

8. *Estoy a tope con el trabajo esta semana.* [es•TOI a TOH•pe kon el tra•BA•ho es•ta se•MAH•na] — I'm swamped with work this week.

9. *Ese plan suena chévere, ¿cómo vas con los preparativos?* [EH•se plan SWE•na CHE•ve•re, KOH•mo vas kon los pre•pa•ra•TEE•vos] — That plan sounds cool, how's it going with the preparations?

10. *No pasa nada, podemos planearlo con más calma.* [no PAH•sa NAH•da, po•DEH•mos pla•NEAR•lo kon MAS KAL•ma] — No worries, we can plan it more calmly.

Chapter 3.1 Worksheet

1) Fill in the blanks with the correct Spanish terms or phrases from the lists provided. This worksheet includes terms from cultural nuances in casual conversation, listening for context, common conversational phrases, and chatting with friends and neighbors. Use the phonetic pronunciations as a guide to help you remember the correct answers.

Cultural Nuances in Casual Conversation

- The _____ (*rhythm*) of conversation varies greatly.
- Understanding _____ (*politeness*) is key.
- A common greeting is a light _____ (*hug*) or cheek kiss.
- Showing _____ *warmth*) and _____ (*acceptance*) is important.
- Listening for context is not just about words. It's about grasping the _____ (*message*).
- Pay attention _____ (*body language*) and tone.
- A _____ (*no rush*) attitude might open the door for more conversation.

Common Colloquial Phrases

- What's up?

  _____

- I'm swamped

  _____

- No worries

  _____

- How's the weather today?

  _____

- Are you going to the fair this weekend?

  _____

- It's cool

  _____

- Let's talk more

  _____

2) **Dialogue:** Let's see a conversation between two friends, Carlos and María, incorporating Spanish words and phrases from the topics discussed.

Carlos: _¡Hola, María! ¿Qué tal?_
[O•la, ma•REE•a! ke TAL?]
(Hello, María! How are you?)

María: _¡Hola, Carlos! Bien, gracias. Y tú, ¿cómo vas?_
[O•la, KAR•los! bjen, GRA•sias. i TOO, KOH•mo vas?]
(Hello, Carlos! Good, thanks. And you, how's it going?)

Carlos: Bien también. ¿Qué tal el clima hoy?
[bjen tam•BJEN. KEH tal el KLEE•ma oy?]
(Good as well. How's the weather today?)

María: *Está un poco nublado. Pero, ¿vas a la feria este fin de semana?*
[es•TAH un POH•ko nu•bla•do. PEH•ro, vas a la FEH•ria ES•te fin de se•MAH•na?]
It's a bit cloudy. But are you going to the fair this weekend?

Carlos: *Sí, pensaba ir. Será chévere. ¿Te gustaría acompañarme?*
[SEE, pen•SA•ba ir. se•RAH CHE•ve•re. te gus•ta•REE•a a•com•pa•NYAR•me?]
(Yes, I was thinking of going. It will be cool. Would you like to join me?)

María: *¡Claro que sí! Me encanta la idea.*
[KLA•ro ke SEE! me en•KAN•ta la i•DEH•a.]
(Of course! I love the idea.)

Carlos: *Genial. Después de la feria, podríamos tomar algo en el café. Estoy a tope esta semana, pero el fin de semana estoy libre.*
[he•NJALl. des•pu•ES de la FEH•ria, po•DREE•a•mos to•MAR AL•go en el ka•FEH. es•TOI a TO•pe es•ta se•MA•na, PE•ro el fin de se•MA•na es•TOI LEE•bre.]
(Great. After the fair, we could get something at the café. I'm swamped this week, but I'm free on the weekend.)

María: *Perfecto, necesito relajarme. Ha sido una semana larga.*
[per•FEK•to, ne•se•SEE•to re•la•HAR•me. a SEE•do OO•na se•MA•na LAR•ga.]
(Perfect, I need to relax. It's been a long week.)

218 • BEGINNER'S SPANISH FOR ADULTS:

Carlos: *Sí, entiendo. Cambiando de tema, ¿has visto el nuevo café que abrieron cerca?*
[SEE, en•TJEN•do. kam•BJAN•do de TEH•ma, as VIS•to el NWE•vo ka•FEH ke a•BRJE•ron SER•ka?]
(Yes, I understand. Changing the subject, have you seen the new café they opened nearby?)

María: *No, pero me mola explorar lugares nuevos. ¿Es bueno?*
[no, PE•ro me MO•la eks•plo•RAR lu•GA•res NWE•vos. es BWE•no?]
(No, but I like exploring new places. Is it good?)

Carlos: *Sí, es muy guay. Tienen un ambiente relajado, perfecto para estar en las nubes un rato.*
[SEE, es muwi GWAI. TJE•nen un am•BJEN•te re•la•HA•do, per•FEK•to PAH•ra es•TAR en las NOO•bes un RA•to.]
(Yes, it's very cool. They have a relaxed atmosphere, perfect for daydreaming for a while.)

María: *¡Qué fuerte! Definitivamente, vamos a chequearlo.*
[KEH FWER•te! de•fi•ni•TEE•va•men•te, VAH•mos a che•KEAR•lo.]
That's intense! Definitely, let's check it out.

Carlos: Vale, será un planazo para el fin de semana.
[VA•le, se•RA un pla•NA•tho PA•ra el fin de se•MA•na.]
(Okay, it will be a great plan for the weekend.)

3.2 Professional Interactions: Communicating in the Workplace

In the tapestry of adult life, the workplace serves as a crucial arena for applying and expanding our language skills. When you step into an office or join a virtual meeting in a Spanish-speaking environment, the words you choose and how you communicate can significantly influence your professional relationships and career trajectory.

Workplace Vocabulary Expansion

Diving into the specifics of your field in Spanish can transform your ability to engage with colleagues and clients alike. For instance, if you're in digital marketing, you will need to understand terms like *"mercado objetivo"* (target market), *"estrategia de contenido"* (content strategy) and *"compromiso del usuario"* (user engagement).

Resources:

- Compile a list of key terms relevant to your industry, adding to it as you encounter new concepts.
- Engage in discussions on industry forums or social media groups in Spanish to expand your professional vocabulary.

This method bolsters your professional lexicon and integrates you more deeply into your field's community, opening up opportunities for learning, collaboration and networking.

KEYWORDS/PHRASES AND HOW TO PRONOUNCE THEM:

1. Oficina [o•fee•SEE•na] – (Office)

2. Reunión virtual [reh•oo•nee•ON vir•too•AL] – (Virtual meeting)

3. Mercado objetivo [mer•KAH•doh ob•hek•TEE•voh] – (Target market)

4. Estrategia de contenido [es•tra•teh•HEE•a de kon•te•NEE•doh] – (Content strategy)

5. Compromiso del usuario [kom•pro•MEE•so del oo•SUA•ree•oh] – (User's compromise)

6. Colegas [ko•LEH•gahs] – (Colleagues)

7. Clientes [klee•EN•tes] – (Clients)

8. Industria [een•DOOS•tree•ah] – (Industry)

9. Colaboración [ko•lah•bo•rah•SEE•on] – (Collaboration)

10. Oportunidades de aprendizaje [oh•por•too•nee•DAH•des de ah•pren•dee•SAH•heh] – (Learning opportunities)

Additional Vocabulary for Workplace Communication:

11. Proyecto [pro•YEK•toh] – (Proyecto)

12. Desarrollo profesional [deh•sah•RRO•yo pro•fe•syo•NAL] – (Professional development)

13. Reunión de equipo [reh•oo•nee•ON de eh•KEE•po] – (Team meeting)

14. Informe [een•FOR•meh] – (Report)

15. Meta [MEH•tah] – (Goal)

Formal vs. Informal Communication

The dance between formal and informal tones in Spanish hinges on understanding the workplace's cultural fabric. While *"tú"* might suit a start-up's laid-back atmosphere, *"usted"* could be more appropriate in traditional corporate settings. Observing how colleagues address each other can offer valuable cues. Here are some points to consider:

- When in doubt, err on the side of formality until invited otherwise.
- Pay attention to email communications and meeting interactions for guidance on the preferred level of formality.

Adjusting your communication style based on these observations ensures that your interactions are respectful and aligned with workplace norms, the company's and country's culture.

WHEN TO USE USTED AND WHEN TO USE TU:

When to Use "Tú"

- **Informal Situations:** Use *"tú"* when talking to friends, family, peers, children and pets.

- **Among Equals:** If you're of the same age or social status as the person you're speaking with, *"tú"* is often appropriate.
- **Social Media & Casual Texts:** When messaging friends or in casual online interactions, *"tú"* is commonly used.
- **Invited to Do So:** Sometimes, someone might ask you to *"tutear"* (use "tú" with them), indicating they're comfortable with a less formal relationship.

When to Use "Usted"

- **Formal Situations:** Use "usted" in professional settings, with authorities (like police or a judge), or when speaking to someone significantly older or in a position of respect.
- **First Meetings:** When meeting someone for the first time, starting with "usted" is a safe bet until told otherwise.
- **Customer Service:** Whether you provide or receive services, using "usted" shows politeness and respect.
- **Formal Writing:** In letters or emails where a formal tone is required, especially in professional contexts, "usted" is preferred.

Regional Variations

It's important to note that using "tú" and "usted" can vary widely across Spanish-speaking countries and even within different regions of the same country. In some places, "usted" is used more frequently, even in somewhat casual contexts, while in others, "tú" is more common. Paying attention to how others speak and following their lead is a good practice.

Tips for Beginners

- When in doubt, use *"Usted"* If you're unsure which form to use, start with *"usted"* to avoid accidentally being too informal. You can switch to *"tú"* if the other person starts using it or suggests it.
- Pay attention to how others address you and each other. This can give you clues about what's appropriate in different contexts.
- If you're unsure whether to use *"tú"* or *"usted"* with someone, it's perfectly acceptable to ask them which they prefer.

Understanding when to use *"tú"* and *"usted"* is vital to mastering Hispanic etiquette and ensuring your interactions are respectful and appropriate for each situation.

Navigating Professional Meetings

Meetings, the heartbeat of corporate life, demand a nuanced command of language and etiquette to share ideas, report progress and collaborate effectively. Phrases like *"En mi opinión..."* (In my opinion...) or *"¿Podríamos considerar...?"* (Could we consider...?) allow you to contribute thoughtfully. To navigate meetings like a pro:

- Prepare by reviewing the agenda and noting any questions or comments in Spanish.
- Practice summarizing your points or questions to ensure clarity and conciseness.

This preparation boosts your confidence and enhances your contributions, making you a valued participant in the discussion.

KEYWORDS/PHRASES AND HOW TO PRONOUNCE THEM:

1. Reunión [reh•oo•nee•ON] – (Meeting)

2. En mi opinión... [en mee oh•pee•nee•ON] – (In my opinion)

3.   ¿Podríamos   considerar...?   [poh•DREE•ah•mohs kohn•see•deh•RAR?] — 8Could we consider...?)

4. Agenda [ah•HEN•dah] – (Agenda)

- *Refers to the list of items to be discussed in a meeting.*

5. Pregunta [preh•GOON•tah] – (Question)

6. Comentario [koh•men•TAH•ree•oh] – (Comment)

7. Resumen [reh•SOO•men] – (Summary)

8. Claridad [klah•ree•DAHD] – (Clarity)

9. Conciso [kohn•SEE•soh] – (Concise)

10. Contribución [kohn•tree•boo•SYOHN] – (Contribution)

Additional Phrases for Effective Meeting Participation:

11. Estoy de acuerdo... [es•TOI deh ah•KWER•doh] – (I agree...)

12. No estoy seguro/a [noh es•TOI seh•GOO•roh] – (I am not sure)

13. ¿Podría repetir eso? [poh•DREE•ah reh•peh•TEER EH•soh] – (Could you repeat that?)

14. Gracias por compartir [GRAH•see•ahs por kohm•par•TEER] – (Thanks for sharing)

15. ¿Cuál es el próximo paso? [KWAHL es el PROK•see•moh PAH•soh] – (What is the next step?)

Email and Written Communication in Spanish

Emails and texts are vital threads connecting the day's tasks and conversations. Clear, respectful messages in Spanish require understanding structure, tone, and etiquette. Start your emails with a polite greeting, such as *"Estimado/a [Name]"* (Dear [Name]), and conclude with a courteous sign-off, like *"Cordialmente"* (Cordially) or *"Atentamente"* (Sincerely). Key pointers include:

- Use bullet points for clarity when listing items or tasks.
- Keep paragraphs short to enhance readability.
- Consider drafting and reviewing your message before sending it for sensitive topics to ensure an appropriate tone.

Mastering these written nuances streamlines communication and reinforces your professional image. It showcases your attention to detail and respect for the recipient.

In weaving through the fabric of professional interactions within Spanish-speaking work environments, from expanding your industry-specific vocabulary to mastering the art of meeting participation and written correspondence, you pave the way for more meaningful contributions and connections. In these interactions, language becomes more than a tool for communication—it becomes a bridge to understanding, collaboration, and growth in your professional journey.

EXAMPLE EMAIL WITH TRANSLATION:

Here's a simplified guide on composing an introductory email to a coworker in Spanish, including simple phrases and their pronunciations.

Subject: Ideas for the Project

Asunto: Ideas para el Proyecto

Estimado Carlos, (Dear Carlos,)

Espero que estés bien. Tengo ideas para mejorar nuestro proyecto. Quiero hablar sobre ellas.

(I hope you are well. I have ideas to improve our project. I want to talk about them.)

Aquí están mis ideas:

(Here are my ideas:)

1. Más reuniones cada semana. (More meetings every week.)
2. Usar una nueva herramienta para el proyecto. (Use a new tool for the project.)
3. Mejorar la comunicación dentro del equipo. (Better talk inside the team.)

Creo que esto puede ayudar a nuestro trabajo. ¿Podemos hablar más en nuestra próxima reunión?

(I think these can help our work. Can we talk more in our next meeting?)

Espero tus comentarios. (I wait for your thoughts.)

Cordialmente,

(Sincerely,)

Ana

Chapter 3.2 Common Spanish Phrases

1. *¿Vas a la reunión virtual mañana?* [vas ah lah reh•oo•nee•ON vir•too•AL mah•NYAH•nah] — Are you going to the virtual meeting tomorrow?

2. *Nuestro mercado objetivo ha respondido bien a la estrategia de contenido.* [NUES•troh mer•KA•doh ob•hek•TEE•voh ah res•pon•DEE•doh byen ah lah es•tra•TEH•hee•a de kon•te•NEE•doh] — Our target market has responded well to the content strategy.

3. *Los colegas y yo estamos trabajando en una nueva colaboración.* [los ko•LEH•gahs ee yo es•TAH•mos tra•ba•HAN•doh en OO•nah NWE•vah ko•lah•bo•rah•see•ON] — My colleagues and I are working on a new collaboration.

4. *¿Qué opinas sobre ampliar nuestro compromiso del usuario?* [KEH o•PEE•nahs SO•breh am•plee•AR NWES•troh kom•pro•MEE•so del oo•SUA•ree•oh] — What do you think about expanding our user engagement?

5. *Tenemos una reunión sobre oportunidades de aprendizaje la próxima semana.* [teh•NEH•mos OO•nah reh•oo•nee•ON SO•breh oh•por•too•nee•DAH•des de ah•pren•dee•SAH•heh lah PROK•see•mah se•MA•nah] — We have a meeting about learning opportunities next week.

6. *Es importante mantener la claridad en nuestras reuniones.* [es eem•por•TAN•teh man•teh•NER lah klah•ree•DAHD en NWES•trahs

reh•oo•nee•O•nes] — It's important to maintain clarity in our meetings.

7. *En mi opinión, debemos enfocarnos más en la industria de la tecnología.* [en mee oh•pee•nee•ON, deh•BE•mos en•fo•KAR•nos MAS en lah een•DOOS•tree•ah de lah tek•no•lo•HEE•ah] — In my opinion, we should focus more on the technology industry.

8. *¿Podríamos considerar nuevas estrategias de contenido para el próximo año?* [poh•DREE•ah•mohs kohn•see•deh•RAR NWE•vahs es•tra•TEH•hee•as de kon•te•NEE•doh PAH•rah el PROK•see•moh AH•nyoh] — Could we consider new content strategies for the coming year?

9. *Estoy de acuerdo con la propuesta, pero necesitamos más investigación.* [es•TOI deh ah•KWER•doh kon lah proh•PWES•tah, PEH•roh ne•seh•see•TAH•mos MAS een•vehs•tee•gah•see•ON] — I agree with the proposal, but we need more research.

10. *Gracias por compartir tus ideas; realmente aportan claridad al proyecto.* [GRAH•see•ahs por kom•par•TEER toos ee•DEH•ahs; reh•AL•men•teh ah•POR•tahn klah•ree•DAHD ahl proh•YEK•toh] — Thank you for sharing your ideas; they truly bring clarity to the project.

3.3 Travel Talk: Engaging with Locals and Making New Friends

Traveling through Spanish-speaking lands offers a wide variety of experiences, with each interaction adding a layer of richness to your adventures. To truly soak in the essence of these places, having a toolkit of phrases for connecting with locals transforms your trip from a mere visit into a journey of meaningful exchanges.

Essential Phrases for Travelers

Navigating conversations with locals takes your experience as a traveler to a next level beyond tourism. Key phrases to have in your arsenal include:

- **Asking for Recommendations:** *"¿Cuál es tu lugar favorito aquí?"* (What's your favorite place here?).
- **Sharing Travel Experiences:** *"Recién visité..."* (I recently visited...).
- **Expressing Gratitude:** *"Estoy agradecido/a por tu ayuda"* (I'm grateful for your help).

Sprinkling these phrases throughout your conversations enhances your ability to communicate and deepens your connection with the people you meet.

KEYWORDS/PHRASES AND HOW TO PRONOUNCE THEM:

1. *¿Cuál es tu lugar favorito aquí?* [KWAHL es too

loo•GAHR fah•voh•REE•toh ah•KEE?] — (What's your favorite place here?)

2. *Recién visité...* [reh•SYEN vee•see•TEH...] — (I recently visited...)

3. *Estoy agradecido/a por tu ayuda* [es•TOI ah•grah•deh•SEE•doh por too ah•YOO•dah] — (I'm grateful for your help)

4. *¿Puedes recomendarme...?* [PWEH•des reh•koh•mehn•DAR•meh...?] — (Can you recommend me...?)

5. *Me gustaría conocer...* [meh goos•tah•REE•ah koh•noh•SER...] — (I would like to know...)

6. *¿Qué me recomiendas?* [KEH meh reh•koh•mee•EN•dahs?] — (What do you recommend?)

7. *¿Cómo llego a...?* [KOH•moh YE•go ah...?] — (How do I get to...?)

8. *Esta es mi primera vez aquí.* [es•TAH es mee pree•MEH•rah vehz ah•KEE.] — (This is my first time here.)

9. *Me encanta este lugar.* [meh en•KAN•tah ES•teh loo•GAHR.] — (I love this place.)

10. *¿Cuál es la especialidad de la casa?* [KWAHL es lah es•peh•syah•lee•DAHD deh lah KAH•sah?] — (What is the house specialty?)

Cultural Sensitivity and Awareness

Understanding the cultural tapestry of the places you visit ensures that your attempts to connect are received with warmth. Key aspects include:

- **Personal Space:** Recognize that concepts of personal space vary. In many Spanish-speaking countries, conversations happen at a closer physical distance than you might be used to.
- **Initiating Conversations:** A simple smile or nod can be the perfect opener before using your Spanish phrases. It signals friendliness and respect, paving the way for a warm interaction.
- **Mindful Observations:** Commenting positively on local traditions, food, or music shows respect for the culture. "Me encanta la música local" (I love the local music) can be a great conversation starter.

Navigating these cultural nuances with sensitivity enriches your travel experience and ensures your engagement efforts are met with openness and enthusiasm.

KEYWORDS/PHRASES AND HOW TO PRONOUNCE THEM:

1. *Espacio personal* [es•PA•syo per•so•NAHL] — (Personal space)
2. *Conversaciones cercanas* [kon•ver•sa•sy•O•nes ser•KA•nas] — (Close conversations)
3. *Sonrisa* [son•REE•sah] — (Smile)
4. *Respeto* [res•PEH•toh] — (Respect)
5. *Interacción cálida* [in•te•rak•sy•ON KA•lee•dah] — (Warm interaction)
6. *Tradiciones locales* [tra•dee•sy•O•nes lo•KAH•les] — (Local traditions)

7. *La comida local* [lah ko•MEE•dah lo•KAHL] —
   (The local food)
8. *Me encanta la música local* [meh en•KAN•tah lah
   MOO•see•kah lo•KAHL] — (I love the local music)
9. *Observaciones conscientes* [ob•ser•va•SYO•nes
   kon•SYEN•tes] — (Mindful observations)
10. *Iniciar una conversación* [ee•nee•SYAR OO•nah
    kon•ver•sa•sy•ON] — (To start a conversation)

Overcoming Language Barriers

Even with a limited vocabulary, there are creative ways to
bridge the language gap, ensuring you can communicate
effectively and connect with those around you:

- **Gestures and Mimicry:** Universal gestures can help
  convey basic needs or emotions, complementing
  verbal communication attempts.
- **Drawings and Pictures:** Sometimes, a quick sketch
  or showing a photo on your phone can help explain
  what words cannot.
- **Technology Aids:** Translation apps or phrasebooks
  on your phone can be invaluable tools for
  navigating more complex conversations or
  understanding directions.

Employing these strategies reduces the stress of language
barriers, making every interaction an opportunity for
learning and connection rather than a challenge to
overcome.

Here are a few practical situations where you can use these strategies to overcome language barriers:

1. Gestures and Mimicry

- **Situation:** You're at a restaurant in a Spanish-speaking country and need to ask where the bathroom is.
- **Strategy:** You can complement your verbal question, *"¿Dónde está el baño?"* with the universal gesture of crossing your legs, which most people understand signifies the need for a restroom.
- **Explanation:** Even if your pronunciation isn't perfect, the gesture can help convey your need.

2. Drawings and Pictures

- **Situation:** You want to buy a specific item, such as a type of fruit, but you need to learn the word for it in Spanish.
- **Strategy:** Use your phone to show a picture of the item or draw it on paper.
- **Explanation:** This visual aid can instantly clarify what you're trying to find, bypassing the need for the correct vocabulary.

3. Technology Aids

- **Situation:** You're trying to explain to a local that you are allergic to a particular food.

- **Strategy:** Use a translation app to translate your dietary restriction and show it to the waiter or store clerk.
- **Explanation:** This ensures that the critical information is accurately communicated and can be understood despite the language difference.

4. Phrasebooks or Language Apps

- **Situation:** You need to ask for directions to a hotel or a tourist attraction.
- **Strategy:** Carry a phrasebook or have a language app ready with common questions and phrases you can point to when asking locals for help.
- **Explanation:** This not only helps you ask the question in the local language but also aids in understanding the response if they reply using words from the same phrasebook or app.

5. Non-Verbal Communication

- **Situation:** You're purchasing something at a market and must negotiate the price.
- **Strategy:** Communicate numbers using hand signals or show the amount you're willing to pay using the calculator on your phone.
- **Explanation:** This can effectively convey numbers and prices when verbal communication may lead to confusion.

In each of these situations, the goal is to find a way to communicate that doesn't rely solely on having a complete command of the language. By being prepared with a mix of gestures, visual aids, and technology, you can navigate through language barriers with greater ease and confidence.

Building Lasting Connections

The friendships forged during travels can add a profound dimension to your experiences, turning fleeting moments into cherished connections:

- **Deepening Conversations:** Once basic communication is established, ask open-ended questions about local life, such as *"¿Cómo es vivir aquí?"* (What's it like living here?) invites more in-depth discussions.
- **Exchanging Contact Information:** Sharing social media handles or email addresses keeps the door open for future communication. *"¿Te puedo agregar en Instagram?"* (Can I add you on Instagram?) is a simple way to stay in touch.
- **Follow-Up:** Sending a message or photo from your travels as a follow-up can strengthen the bond, showing genuine interest in maintaining the connection.

These efforts to build and maintain connections with locals and fellow travelers enrich your journey, turning it into a set of shared experiences and friendships that span the globe.

In navigating the art of travel talk, from mastering essential phrases to understanding cultural cues and employing creative strategies to overcome language barriers, you weave yourself into the local fabric, transforming your travel experience. Engaging with locals and making new friends along the way opens up a world of possibilities, where every conversation is a doorway to deeper understanding, and every interaction leaves a lasting imprint on your heart. Through these exchanges, you discover the beauty of new places and the shared humanity that connects us all, no matter where we roam.

Spanish Cultural Values Regarding Friendships:

1. *Confianza* (Trustworthiness): Trust is the foundation of any strong friendship, and Hispanic cultures values building relationships with a solid trust base.
2. *Sinceridad* (Sincerity): Being open, honest, and genuine is highly valued. Pretense is generally frowned upon, and people appreciate it when you are straightforward.
3. *Buena comunicación* (Good Communication): It is essential to talk openly, share feelings, and discuss problems.
4. *Respeto* (Respect): Respect for each other's opinions, lifestyles, and personal space is crucial, even if there is a close physical proximity in social settings.
5. *Lealtad* (Loyalty): It is highly regarded that people stand by each other through good and bad times and show loyalty to their friends.

6. *Intereses comunes* (Shared Interests): As with any culture, sharing common hobbies, tastes in music, food, or other interests can be the glue that binds friends together.

7. *Alegría y sentido del humor* (Joyfulness and a Sense of Humor): Hispanics often enjoy humor and laughter, and a good sense of humor can be an essential trait in a friend.

8. *Apoyo* (Supportiveness): Friends are expected to offer support and help whenever necessary, whether for personal or professional matters.

9. *Calidez y afecto* (Warmth and Affection): Physical touch, such as hugs and kisses on the cheek are common among friends and signify warmth and affection.

10. *Sociabilidad* (Sociability): Being sociable and willing to participate in social activities is often important, as many Hispanic social activities revolve around group gatherings.

Remember, these are generalizations, and individual preferences can vary. The key to any friendship is getting to know the person and understanding what they value in their relationship with others.

Chapter 3.3 Common Spanish Phrases

1. *¿Cuál es tu lugar favorito aquí?* [KWAHL es too loo•GAHR fah•voh•REE•toh ah•KEE] — What's your favorite place here?

2. *Recién visité el museo local y fue increíble.* [reh•SYEN vee•see•TEH el moo•SEH•oh loh•KAHL ee fweh een•kreh•EE•bleh] — I recently visited the local museum and it was incredible.

3. *Estoy agradecido por tu ayuda con las direcciones.* [es•TOI ah•grah•deh•SEE•doh por too ah•YOO•dah kon las dee•rek•see•O•nes] — I'm grateful for your help with the directions.

4. *¿Puedes recomendarme un buen restaurante aquí?* [PWEH•des reh•koh•mehn•DAR•meh oon BWEN res•tow•RAHN•teh ah•KEE?] — Can you recommend a good restaurant here?

5. *Me gustaría conocer más sobre las tradiciones locales.* [meh goos•tah•REE•ah koh•noh•SER MAHS SO•breh las tra•dee•sy•O•nes loh•KAH•les] — I would like to know more about local traditions.

6. *¿Qué me recomiendas hacer este fin de semana?* [KEH meh reh•koh•mee•EN•dahs ah•SER ES•teh feen de se•MAH•nah?] — What do you recommend I do this weekend?

7. *¿Cómo llego al parque central desde aquí?* [KOH•moh YE•go ahl PAHR•keh sen•TRAHL DEHS•deh ah•KEE?] — How do I get to the central park from here?

8. *Esta es mi primera vez en esta ciudad.* [ES•tah es mee pree•MEH•rah VEHZ en es•TAH see•oo•DAHD] — This is my first time in this city.

9. *Me encanta este café por su atmósfera acogedora.* [meh en•KAHN•tah ES•teh kah•FEH por soo aht•MOHS•feh•rah ah•koh•heh•DOH•rah] — I love this café for its cozy atmosphere.

10. *¿Cuál es la especialidad de la casa en este restaurante?*
    [KWAHL es lah es•peh•syah•lee•DAHD deh lah
    KAH•sah en ES•teh res•tow•RAHN•teh] — What
    is the house specialty in this restaurant?

Chapter 3.3 Worksheet

Fill in the blanks with the correct Spanish terms from the lists provided. This worksheet is designed to help you practice phrases that are useful for overcoming language barriers, demonstrating cultural sensitivity and awareness, and engaging with locals to make new friends.

Overcoming Language Barriers

- When you don't know the word in Spanish, you can use your phone to show a
  _____(*picture*).
- If you are lost,
  a_____(*translation app*) on your phone can help you ask for directions.
- To communicate numbers, you might use_____(*gestures*)
  or a
  _____(*calculator*).

Cultural Sensitivity and Awareness

- To comment positively on local customs, you might say, "*Me encanta la
  _____(music)
  local.*"

- When you meet someone, be mindful of the
  _____(*personal
  space*), which might be closer than you're used to.
- Acknowledging
  local_____(*food*)
  is a way to show respect for the culture.

Engaging with Locals and Making New Friends

- To find the best spots in town, you could ask, "*¿Cuál
  es
  tu_____(place)
  favorito aquí?*"
- When sharing your travel stories, you might start
  with
  "*Recién_____(I
  visited)...*"
- Showing gratitude can be done by saying,
  "*Estoy_____(grateful)
  por tu ayuda*".

3.4 Expressing Opinions: Sharing Your Thoughts and Feelings

When navigating the lively world of Spanish-speaking cultures, articulating your thoughts and emotions enriches your interactions and bridges the gap between mere communication and meaningful conversation. Whether you're savoring a delicious meal, debating a hot topic or simply talking about your day, the richness of your language enhances the depth of your connections.

Vocabulary for Opinions and Emotions

Expanding your vocabulary to include a broad spectrum of emotions and opinions transforms simple exchanges into complex dialogues. Words like *"contento/a"* (happy), *"decepcionado/a"* (disappointed), *"interesante"* (interesting), and *"preocupante"* (worrisome) allow you to convey your feelings with precision. When sharing your viewpoint you may use phrases like *"A mi parecer..."* (In my opinion...) or *"Desde mi punto de vista..."* (From my point of view...) to introduce your thoughts without imposing them on the listener.

- **Tip:** Build a personal dictionary of emotions and opinion phrases, adding examples of when you felt or thought something similar. This personal touch makes recalling these words easier when you need them.

1. Contento/a — (Happy)

- **Male:** [kon•TEN•toh]
- **Female:** [kon•TEN•tah]

2. Decepcionado/a — (Disappointed)

- **Male:** [de•sep•syo•NAH•doh]
- **Female:** [de•sep•syo•NAH•dah]

3. Interesante [in•te•re•SAHN•teh] — (Interesting)

4. Preocupante [pre•oh•koo•PAHN•teh] — (Worrisome)

5. *A mi parecer...* [ah mee pah•reh•SER...] — (In my opinion...)

6. *Desde mi punto de vista...* [DES•deh mee POON•toh deh VEES•tah...] — (From my point of view...)

7. *Emocionado/a* — (Excited)

- **Male:** [eh•moh•syo•nah•doh]
- **Female:** [eh•moh•syo•nah•dah]

8. *Frustrado/a* — (Frustrated)

- **Male:** [froos•TRAH•doh]
- **Female:** [froos•TRAH•dah]

9. *Sorprendido/a* — (Surprised)

- **Male:** [sor•pren•DEE•doh]
- **Female:** [sor•pren•DEE•dah]

10. *Agradecido/a* — (Grateful)

- **Male:** [ah•grah•deh•SEE•doh]
- **Female:** [ah•grah•deh•SEE•dah]

Structuring Your Argument

Presenting your views clearly ensures your message is heard and understood. Start with a clear statement of your opinion, follow up with the reasons behind it, and, if necessary, include examples to illustrate your point. This systematic

244 • BEGINNER'S SPANISH FOR ADULTS:

approach aids discussions on any topic, from casual debates on the best local dish to more serious conversations about political or social issues.

- **Practice Technique:** Engage in mock debates on topics you're passionate about with language partners. This safe environment is perfect for practicing structuring your thoughts coherently in Spanish.

KEYWORDS/PHRASES AND HOW TO PRONOUNCE THEM:

1. *Mi opinión es que...* [mee oh•pee•NYON es keh] — (My opinion is that...)
2. *Primero* [pree•MEH•roh] — (First)
3. *Porque* [POR•keh] — (Because)
4. *Además* [ah•deh•MAS] — (Furthermore)
5. *Por ejemplo* [por eh•HEM•ploh] — (For example)
6. *Entonces* [en•TOHN•ses] — (So/Then)
7. *Sin embargo* [seen em•BAHR•goh] — (However)
8. *En conclusión* [en kon•kloo•SYON] — (In conclusion)
9. *Estoy convencido/a de que...* (I am convinced that...)
10. **Male:** [es•TOI kon•ven•SEE•doh deh keh]
11. **Female:** [es•TOI kon•ven•SEE•dah deh keh]
12. *Debate* [deh•BAH•teh] — (Debate)

Agreeing and Disagreeing Politely

Moving through agreement and disagreement in conversations is a skill that fosters respect and openness. Phrases such as *"Estoy de acuerdo contigo en que..."* (I agree with you that...) show concurrence, while *"Entiendo tu punto, pero..."* (I understand your point, but...) introduce a differing perspective gently. This nuanced approach to dialogue ensures that exchanges remain enriching and respectful, even when opinions diverge.

- **Strategy for Practice:** In discussions, challenge yourself to find at least one point you can agree with before presenting a counter-argument. This practice builds empathy and promotes a more balanced exchange of ideas.

KEYWORDS/PHRASES AND HOW TO PRONOUNCE THEM:

1. Estoy de acuerdo contigo en que... [es•TOY deh ah•KWER•doh kon•TEE•goh en keh] — (I agree with you that...)

2. Entiendo tu punto, pero... [en•TYEN•doh too POON•toh, PEH•roh] — (I understand your point, but...)

3. Exactamente [ek•sahk•tah•MEN•teh] — (Exactly)

4. No estoy seguro/a de que... (I am not sure that...)

- **Male:** [no es•TOI seh•GOO•roh deh keh]
- **Female:** [no es•TOI seh•GOO•rah deh keh]

5. Podría ser, pero considera que... [po•DREE•ah ser, PEH•roh kon•see•DEH•rah keh] — (It could be, but consider that...)

6. Tienes razón en parte, sin embargo... [TYEH•nes rah•SON en PAR•teh, seen em•BAR•goh] — (You are partly right, however...)

7. Respeto tu opinión, pero... [res•PEH•toh too oh•pee•NYON, PEH•roh...] — (I respect your opinion, but...)

8. Veo lo que dices, pero... [VEH•oh loh keh DEE•ces, PEH•roh...] — (I see what you're saying, but...)

9. Es una perspectiva interesante, no obstante... [es OO•nah pers•pehk•TEE•vah in•te•re•SAHN•teh, noh obs•TAHN•teh] — (It's an interesting perspective, none-theless...)

10. Coincido en ciertos aspectos, pero... [koh•een•SEE•doh en SYER•tos as•PEK•tos, PEH•roh...] — (I agree on certain aspects, but...)

Cultural Perspectives on Debates

The approach to debates and discussions can vary significantly across cultures, with some societies favoring directness and others preferring more subtle methods of disagreement. Understanding these cultural nuances is critical to engaging effectively and respectfully. For example, in some cultures, openly challenging someone's opinion, especially in a public setting, might be seen as confrontational, while in others, it's a sign of an engaged and lively discussion.

- **Cultural Insight Exercise:** Research a hot topic in a specific Spanish-speaking country and observe online discussions to see how people express their opinions and respond to others. Note the phrases used and the overall tone of the debate.

Incorporating these elements into your Spanish repertoire enhances your ability to express yourself and deepens your cultural understanding and empathy. The art of conversation lies not just in speaking but in connecting, empathizing and respecting different types of thought and feelings.

KEYWORDS/PHRASES AND HOW TO PRONOUNCE THEM:

1. Debate [de•BA•te] — (Debate)

2. Discusión [dis•ku•SJON] — (Discussion)

3. Directo [di•REK•to] — (Direct)

4. Indirecto [in•di•REK•to] — (Indirect)

5. Confrontacional — (Confrontational)

- [kon•fron•ta•theeo•NAL] (Spain)
- [kon•fron•ta•sjo•NAL] (Latin America)

6. Respeto [res•PE•to] — (Respect)

7. Cultura [kul•TOO•ra] — (Culture)

8. Opinión [o•pi•NJON] — (Opinion)

9. *Tono de debate* [TO•no de de•BA•te] — (Tone of the debate)

10. *Empatía* [em•pa•TEE•a] — (Empathy)

11. *Perspectiva cultural* [pers•pek•TEE•va kul•tu•RAL] — (Cultural perspective)

12. *Expresión de ideas* [eks•pre•SJON de i•DEH•as] — (Expression of ideas)

13. *Entender las diferencias* — (Understanding differences)

- [en•ten•DER las di•fe•REN•theeas/] (Spain)
- [en•ten•der las di•fe•ren•SJAS] (Latin America)

14. *Conexión humana* [ko•nek•SJON u•MA•na] — (Human connection)

Chapter 3.4 Common Spanish Phrases

1. *Estoy contento por la oportunidad de discutir este tema.*
   [es•TOI kon•TEN•toh por lah
   oh•por•too•nee•DAHD deh dees•koo•TEER
   ES•teh TEH•mah] — (I'm happy about the
   opportunity to discuss this topic.)

2. *A mi parecer, la cultura influye mucho en nuestras
   opiniones.* [ah mee pah•reh•SER, lah
   kool•TOO•rah een•FLOO•yeh MOO•choh en
   NWES•trahs oh•pee•NYO•nes] — (In my opinion,
   culture greatly influences our opinions.)

3. *Me siento emocionado por aprender sobre diferentes
   perspectivas culturales.* [meh en•KWNE•troh

eh•moh•syo•NAH-doh deh ah•prehn•DER deh
dee•feh•REN•tes pers•pehk•TEE•vas
kool•too•RAH•les] — (I'm excited to learn from
different cultural perspectives.)

4. *Desde mi punto de vista, el respeto es fundamental en
cualquier debate.* [DES•deh mee POOHN•toh deh
VEES•tah, el res•PEH•toh es
foon•dah•men•TAHL en kwal•KYEHR
deh•BAH•teh] — (From my point of view, respect is
fundamental in any debate.)

5. *Estoy agradecido por este intercambio de ideas.*
[es•TOI ah•grah•deh•SEE•doh por ES•teh
een•ter•KAHM•byoh deh ee•DEH•as] — (I'm
grateful for this exchange of ideas.)

6. *Me gustaría conocer tu opinión sobre este asunto.* [meh
goos•tah•REE•ah koh•noh•SER too
oh•pee•NYON SOH•breh ES•teh ah•SOON•toh]
— (I would like to know your opinion on this
matter.)

7. *Estoy convencido de que podemos encontrar un punto
medio.* [es•TOI kon•ven•SEE•doh deh keh
poh•DEH•mos ehn•kohn•TRAR oon POOHN•toh
MEH•dyo] — (I am convinced that we can find a
middle ground.)

8. *Este debate ha sido muy interesante y enriquecedor.*
[ES•teh deh•BAH•teh ah SEE•doh MOO•ee
een•te•re•SAHN•teh ee ehn•ree•keh•seh•DOR]
— (This debate has been very interesting and
enriching.)

9. *¿Cuál es la especialidad de la casa en términos de
opinión?* [KWAHL es lah es•peh•syah•lee•DAHD

deh lah KAH•sah en TEHR•mee•nos deh
oh•pee•NYON?] — (What is the house specialty in
terms of opinion?)

10. *Entiendo tu punto, pero tengo una perspectiva
diferente.* [en•TYEN•doh too POOHN•toh,
PEH•roh TEN•goh OO•nah pers•pehk•TEE•vah
dee•feh•REN•teh] — (I understand your point, but
I have a different perspective.)

Chapter 3.4 Worksheet

Fill in the blanks with the correct Spanish terms from the
lists provided. This worksheet is designed to help you practice phrases that help you engage in debates, agree and
disagree politely, structure arguments, and share thoughts
and opinions.

Cultural Perspectives on Debates

- Understanding _____ (*cultural
  nuances*) is key to engaging effectively.
- In some cultures, being _____ (*direct*)
  is seen as confrontational.
- It's important to have _____ (*respect*) in
  every discussion.

Agreeing and Disagreeing Politely

- I agree with you that... becomes
  _____(*Estoy
  de acuerdo contigo en que...*) in Spanish.

- To introduce a differing perspective gently, you might say

  _____(*Entiendo tu punto, pero...*).

Structuring Your Argument

- First, state your opinion clearly with

  _____(*Mi opinión es que...*)
- Then, support your opinion with reasons, starting with

  _____(*Primero*).

Sharing Your Thoughts and Opinions

- When expressing happiness, you might say

  _____(*contento/a*).
- If you find something interesting, you can say

  _____(*interesante*).

3.5 Problem-Solving: Handling Conflicts and Resolving Issues in Spanish

Conflicts and challenges are partners we must occasionally embrace in daily life. Navigating these moments in Spanish-speaking environments can significantly influence outcomes and relationships. This section provides tools and perspectives for effective conflict resolution, negotiation, and making amends, all while respecting the cultural backdrop that colors these interactions.

Language for Conflict Resolution

When misunderstandings and disagreements surface, having a toolkit of phrases can guide us to resolution with dignity and respect. Phrases such as *"Creo que hay un malentendido"* (I think there's a misunderstanding) or *"Vamos a encontrar una solución juntos"* (Let's find a solution together) set a cooperative tone. Here are some steps to consider:

- Start by clarifying the issue and seeking to understand it before being understood.
- Express your perspective or feelings about the situation using "I" statements to avoid placing blame, such as *"Me siento..."* (I feel...).
- Invite the other party to share their viewpoint, showing a willingness to listen, with *"¿Cuál es tu opinión?"* (What's your opinion?).

These strategies facilitate constructive dialogue and reinforce mutual respect, a cornerstone of effective conflict resolution.

KEYWORDS/PHRASES AND HOW TO PRONOUNCE THEM:

1. *Malentendido* [ma•len•ten•DEE•doh] — (Misunderstanding)
2. *Creo que hay un malentendido* [KRE•oh keh ai oon ma•len•ten•DEE•doh] — (I think there's a misunderstanding)

3. *Vamos a encontrar una solución juntos* [VAH•mos a en•kon•TRAR OO•na so•loo•SYON HOON•tos] — (Let's find a solution together)
4. *Me siento...* [me SJEN•toh...] — (I feel...)
5. *¿Cuál es tu opinión?* [KWAHL es too oh•pee•NJON?] — (What's your opinion?)
6. *Sin culpar* [sin kool•PAR] — (Without blaming)
7. *Diálogo constructivo* [dee•AH•lo•go kons•truk•TEE•vo] — (Constructive dialogue)
8. *Respeto mutuo* [res•PEH•to MOO•tw•o] — (Mutual respect)
9. *Negociación* [ne•go•sjee•a•SYON] — (Negotiation)
10. *Hacer las paces* [a•SER las PAH•ses] — (To make amends)

Negotiating Terms and Conditions

Negotiations, whether sealing a business deal or deciding on a family dinner spot, require clear communication and a spirit of compromise. Key phrases such as *"¿Qué te parece si...?"* (What if we...?) or *"Podemos llegar a un acuerdo"* (We can reach an agreement) help steer discussions towards mutually beneficial outcomes. Remember:

- Be clear about your needs and limits, but remain open to alternatives.
- Use questions to explore options and show openness, like *"¿Hay alguna alternativa que funcione para ambos?"* (Is there an alternative that works for both of us?).

This approach not only aids in reaching agreements but also strengthens relationships by demonstrating flexibility and consideration for others' needs.

KEYWORDS/PHRASES AND HOW TO PRONOUNCE THEM:

1. *Negociaciones* [ne•go•sjeea•SJO•nes] — (Negotiations)
2. *¿Qué te parece si...?* [KEH te pa•RE•se si...] — (What if we...?)
3. *Podemos llegar a un acuerdo* [po•DE•mos ye•GAR a oon ah•KWER•do] — (We can reach an agreement)
4. *Necesidades* [ne•se•si•DA•des] — (Needs)
5. *Límites* [LEE•mi•tes] — (Limits)
6. *Alternativas* [al•ter•na•TEE•vas] — (Alternatives)
7. *¿Hay alguna alternativa que funcione para ambos?* [ai al•GOO•na al•ter•na•TEE•va ke fun•SJO•ne PA•ra AM•bos] — (Is there an alternative that works for both of us?)
8. *Compromiso* [kom•pro•MEE•so] — (Compromise)
9. *Flexibilidad* [flek•si•bi•li•DAHD] — (Flexibility)
10. *Consideración* [kon•si•de•ra•SJON] — (Consideration)

Strategies for Conflict Resolution in a Spanish-Speaking Environment:

- **Be Clear and Respectful:** Start negotiations by clearly expressing your *necesidades* (needs) and

límites (limtis) but remain open to hearing the other
party's needs and limits.

- **Seek Common Ground:** Use phrases like *¿Qué te
parece si...?* (What do you think if...?) to suggest
solutions and find a middle ground.
- **Show Willingness to Compromise:** Demonstrating
flexibilidad (flexibility) and a willingness to make
compromisos (compromises) can often lead to more
favorable outcomes for all parties involved.
- **Maintain a Positive Tone:** Keeping discussions
constructive and using questions to explore
alternativas (alternatives) helps maintain a positive
atmosphere and shows respect for the other party's
viewpoint.
- **Demonstrate Empathy and Understanding:**
Recognizing and validating the other person's
feelings and positions can foster an environment of
mutual *consideración* (consideration), which is
crucial for reaching an agreement.

These strategies and phrases can help you navigate negotiations and conflict resolutions effectively, fostering a spirit of
cooperation and mutual respect.

Apologizing and Making Amends

An apology can be a powerful tool for healing and restoring
harmony. In Spanish, saying *"Lo siento"* (I'm sorry) is just the
beginning. To truly make amends, consider:

- Be specific about what you're apologizing for to demonstrate understanding of the impact, such as *"Lo siento por llegar tarde"* (I'm sorry for being late).
- Offering to make things right, with phrases like *"¿Cómo puedo arreglarlo?"* (How can I make it right?).

A sincere apology and actions to rectify the situation can rebuild trust and show genuine remorse, which are essential steps in moving forward from conflict.

KEYWORDS/PHRASES AND HOW TO PRONOUNCE THEM:

1. *Lo siento* [loh SYEN•toh] — (I'm sorry)
2. *Lo siento por llegar tarde* [loh SYEN•toh pohr ye•GAR TAR•deh] — (I'm sorry for being late)
3. *¿Cómo puedo arreglarlo?* [KO•mo PWE•do a•rre•GLAR•loh] — (How can I make it right?)
4. *Perdóname* [per•DO•na•meh] — (Forgive me)
5. *Fue un error* [FWEH oon eh•RROR] — (It was a mistake)
6. *No volverá a ocurrir* [noh bol•ve•RAH ah oh•coo•RREER] — (It won't happen again)
7. *Quiero enmendarlo* [KYE•roh en•men•DAR•loh] — (I want to make amends)
8. *Acepta mis disculpas* [ah•SEP•tah mees dees•COOL•pahs] — (Accept my apologies)
9. *Me arrepiento* [meh ah•rreh•PYEN•toh] — (I regret it)
10. *¿Podemos hablar sobre ello?* [po•DEH•mos ah•BLAR SO•breh EH•yoh] — (Can we talk about it?)

Cultural Attitudes Towards Conflict

Understanding how conflicts are viewed and handled across Spanish-speaking cultures can enhance our approach to resolution. Some cultures may value directness and open discussion of issues, while others prefer subtlety and indirect methods to avoid confrontation. Key insights include:

- In some contexts, maintaining harmony can be more important than addressing the conflict head-on.
- The role of mediators or third parties can be prevalent, offering a neutral ground for resolving disputes.

Being mindful of these cultural nuances ensures that our efforts to solve problems are respectful and effective, aligning with local values and communication styles.

By weaving these strategies into our interactions, we navigate the choppy waters of conflict with grace and effectiveness. The goal is not merely to solve the immediate problem but to foster understanding, respect and cooperation. In doing so, we resolve individual disputes and contribute to building better relationships that can withstand the tests of time and challenge.

As we wrap up this exploration into problem-solving and conflict resolution, we're reminded of the power of communication, empathy, and cultural awareness in overcoming challenges. These tools help us navigate difficult conversations and deepen our connections with others, laying the groundwork for more meaningful and harmonious interactions. As we move forward, let us carry these lessons into all aspects of our lives, ready to face challenges with confidence, understanding, and a spirit of cooperation.

Strategies for Conflict Resolution:

1. Emphasize Respect and Courtesy

- *Respeto* (Respect) is paramount in Spanish-speaking cultures. Always approach conflicts with a respectful tone, using polite language. Phrases like *"Por favor"* (Please) and *"Gracias"* (Thank you) can maintain a courteous atmosphere even in disagreement.

2. Use Formal Language When Appropriate

- In many Spanish-speaking cultures, formal language (*usted* instead of *tú*) is used to show respect, especially with people you don't know well, older individuals, or in professional settings.

3. Seek to Understand Before Being Understood

- Show genuine interest in the other person's perspective by asking clarifying questions like *"¿Puede explicarme...?"* (Can you explain...?). Listening actively demonstrates your willingness to resolve the conflict.

4. Express Your Feelings and Needs Clearly

- Use "I" statements to express your feelings and needs without placing blame. For instance, *"Me siento..."* (I feel...) followed by your emotion or need, helps to communicate your side without accusing the other person.

5. Aim for Compromise

- Spanish-speaking cultures often value community and harmony, so finding a middle ground is preferred. Use phrases like *"¿Qué te parece si...?"* (What if we...?) to propose compromises.

6. Be Patient and Show Willingness to Reconcile

- Patience is key in conflict resolution. Show your willingness to make amends and reconcile by saying, *"Quiero arreglar esto"* (I want to fix this). This opens up space for mutual understanding and resolution.

7. Understand the Cultural Context

- Realize that attitudes toward conflict can vary widely among Spanish-speaking countries and even within regions. In some cultures, direct confrontation may be avoided in favor of more indirect methods of expressing disagreement.

8. Apologize Sincerely When Necessary

- If you're in the wrong, offer a sincere apology. *"Lo siento"* (I'm sorry) can go a long way in mending fences. Be specific about what you're apologizing for to show understanding and remorse.

9. Use Neutral Parties or Mediators if Needed

- In some situations, involving a neutral third party to mediate the conflict can be helpful, especially in formal or business disputes. This can help ensure that both sides are heard and respected.

10. Reflect on the Experience

- After resolving the conflict, reflect on the experience and what you've learned. This reflection can enhance your cultural competence and prepare you for future interactions.

Effective conflict resolution in Spanish is not just about speaking the language; it's about understanding and respecting the cultural nuances that influence how people communicate and relate.

Chapter 3.5 Common Spanish Phrases

1. *Creo que hay un malentendido entre nosotros.*
   [KRE•oh keh ai oon ma•len•ten•DEE•doh EN•tre
   no•SO•tros] — I think there's a misunderstanding
   between us.

2. *Vamos a encontrar una solución juntos para resolver
   esto.* [VA•mos a en•kon•TRAR OO•na
   so•loo•SYON HOON•tos PAH•rah re•sol•VER
   ES•to] — Let's find a solution together to resolve
   this

3. *Me siento frustrado, pero estoy dispuesto a dialogar.*
   [me SJEN•toh froos•TRA•doh, PEH•roh es•TOI
   dis•PWES•toh a dee•ah•lo•GAR] — I feel
   frustrated, but I am willing to talk.

4. *¿Cuál es tu opinión sobre lo que sucedió?* [KWAHL es
   too oh•pee•NJON SO•bre lo ke soo•se•DJO] —
   What's your opinion about what happened?

5. *Busquemos un diálogo constructivo sin culpar a nadie.*
   [bus•KE•mos oon dee•AH•lo•go
   kons•truk•TEE•vo sin KOOL•par a NA•dje] —
   Let's seek a constructive dialogue without blaming
   anyone.

6. *Necesitamos mostrar respeto mutuo durante nuestras
   negociaciones.* [ne•se•si•TAH•mos mos•TRAR
   res•PE•to MOO•tw•o doo•RAN•te nwes•TRAS
   ne•go•sjee•a•SJO•nes] — We need to show mutual
   respect during our negotiations.

7. *¿Hay alguna alternativa que funcione para ambos?
   Busquemos compromisos.* [eye al•GOO•na
   al•ter•na•TEE•va ke fun•SJO•ne pa•ra AM•bos?

bus•KE•mos kom•pro•MEE•sos] — Is there an alternative that works for both of us? Let's look for compromises.

8. *Lo siento por cualquier malentendido que haya causado.* [loh SYEN•toh pohr kwal•KYER ma•len•ten•DEE•doh ke AH•ja kow•SA•do] — I'm sorry for any misunderstanding I may have caused.

9. *Quiero enmendarlo y demostrar mi compromiso con el equipo.* [KYE•roh en•men•DAR•loh ee de•mos•TRAR mee kom•pro•MEE•so kon el eh•KEE•po] — I want to make amends and show my commitment to the team.

10. *Perdóname por mi reacción; no volverá a ocurrir.* [per•DO•na•meh pohr mee re•ahk•SJON; noh bol•ve•RAH ah oh•coo•RREER] — Forgive me for my reaction; it won't happen again.

Chapter 3.5 Worksheet

1) Fill in the blanks with the correct Spanish terms from the lists provided. This worksheet is designed to help you practice phrases that help you apologize, make amends, negotiate terms and conditions, problem-solve, handle conflicts, and resolve issues.

Apologizing and Making Amends

- I'm sorry for being late translates to

- How can I make it right? is asked as

  _____

- To offer forgiveness, you might say

  _____

Negotiating Terms and Conditions

- What if we...? can be posed as

  _____

- We can reach an agreement is expressed by

  _____

- Is there an alternative that works for both of us? Is asked as

  _____

Problem Solving, and Handling Conflicts and Resolving Issues

- I think there's a misunderstanding translates to

  _____

- Let's find a solution together translates to

  _____

- What's your opinion? Translates to

  _____

2) **Dialogue:** Here's a simplified conversation between two coworkers, Juan and Marta, incorporating phrases related to apologizing, negotiating terms and conditions, and problem-solving.

Juan: *Hola, Marta. Lo siento por llegar tarde.*
[loh SYEN•toh pohr ye•GAR TAR•deh]
(Hello, Marta. I'm sorry for being late.)

Marta: *Está bien, Juan. ¿Cómo podemos arreglarlo?*
[KOH•moh po•DEH•mos arreh•GLAR•loh]
(It's okay, Juan. How can we make it right?)

Juan: *Podemos llegar a un acuerdo. Trabajaré una hora extra hoy.*
[po•DEH•mos ye•GAR a oon ah•KWER•doh.
tra•ba•ha•RE OO•nah OH•rah EKS•tra oy.)
(We can reach an agreement. I will work an extra hour today.)

Marta: *Me parece bien. Pero, ¿cuál es tu opinión sobre el proyecto?*
[me pa•REH•se byen. PEH•ro, KWAHL es too
oh•pee•NYON SO•breh el pro•YEK•toh?]

(That sounds good to me. But what's your opinion about the project?)

Juan: *Creo que hay un malentendido. Yo pensé que la fecha de entrega era la próxima semana.*
[KRE•oh ke ai oon ma•len•ten•DEE•doh. yo pen•SE ke la FE•cha de en•TRE•ga EH•rah la PROK•see•mah se•MA•nah.]
(I think there's a misunderstanding. I thought the deadline was next week.)

Marta: *Entiendo. Vamos a encontrar una solución juntos. ¿Qué te parece si revisamos el calendario ahora?*
[en•TYEN•doh. VA•mos a en•kon•TRAR OO•nah so•loo•SYON HOON•tos. KEH te pa•RE•se see re•vi•SA•mos el ka•len•DA•ryo ah•OH•rah]
(I understand. Let's find a solution together. What if we check the calendar now?)

Juan: *Me parece una buena idea. Gracias por tu comprensión.*
[me pa•RE•se OO•nah BWE•na ee•DE•ah. GRA•syas pohr too kom•pren•SYON]
(That sounds like a good idea. Thank you for your understanding.)

Marta: *De nada, Juan. Es importante trabajar en equipo.*
[de NAH•dah, hwan. es im•por•TAHN•te tra•ba•HAR en eh•KEE•po]
(You're welcome, Juan. It's important to work as a team.)

FOUR

Navigating the Waters of Influence: The Spanish of Persuasion and Negotiation

I imagine you're at a bustling street market in Buenos Aires or a sleek startup office in Barcelona. Here, the air crackles with potential: deals to be struck, minds to be changed, bonds to be forged. Whether haggling over prices or pitching a groundbreaking idea, your success hinges on what you say and how you say it. Welcome to the arena of negotiation and persuasion, where words wield power and being cultural savvy is your best ally.

4.1 Negotiating and Persuading: Getting What You Want

Strategies for Effective Negotiation

Negotiation is a dance. Sometimes, you lead, sometimes, you follow, but always with an eye on that graceful equilibrium where everyone feels like they've won. Preparation is your first step. Know your facts, understand your wants, and, most importantly, recognize what you can flex on. Is it price, time, or features? Each negotiation is unique.

- **Preparation Checklist:** This visual tool lists vital aspects, such as goals, limits, and alternatives. It is helpful to keep on hand during negotiations.

Next, consider the setting. A casual chat over coffee might open doors that a formal boardroom meeting keeps shut. Timing and place matter as much as the words you choose.

When presenting your case, clarity and conciseness are your best friends. Rambling needs to pay more attention; being vague invites misunderstanding. Use phrases like *"Lo que ofrezco es..."* (What I'm offering is...) to state your position confidently and clearly.

But negotiation is a two-way street. Listening is as valuable as speaking. Questions like *"¿Cuál es tu opinión?"* (What is your opinion?) show respect and openness, inviting collaboration instead of confrontation.

KEYWORDS/PHRASES AND HOW TO PRONOUNCE THEM:

1. *Negociación* [ne•go•seeah•see•ON] — (Negotiation)
2. *Preparación* [preh•pah•rah•see•ON] — (Preparation)
3. *Objetivos* [ob•heh•TEE•vohs] — (Goals)
4. *Límites* [LEE•mee•tehs] — (Limits)
5. *Alternativas* [ahl•tehr•nah•TEE•vahs] — (Alternatives)

6. *Lo que ofrezco es...* [loh keh oh•FREZ•koh ehs...] — (What I'm offering is...)

7. *¿Cuál es tu opinión?* [KWAHL ehs too oh•pee•nee•ON] — (What is your opinion?)

8. *Flexibilidad* [flehk•see•bee•lee•DAHD] — (Flexibility)

9. *Claridad* [klah•ree•DAHD] — (Clarity)

10. *Conciso* [kon•SEE•soh] — (Concise)

Strategies for Persuasion and Negotiation in Spanish-speaking Cultures:

- **Know Your Facts:** Being well-prepared with *hechos* [EH•chos] (facts) and clear *objetivos* [ob•he•TEE•vos] (objectives) is crucial.

- **Understand Your Flexibility:** Recognize areas where you can apply your *flexibilidad* [flek•see•bee•lee•DAHD] (flexibility), such as price or time.

- **Consider the Setting:** Your negotiation's *ambiente* [am•BYEN•teh] (setting) can significantly affect its outcome. A relaxed environment may be more conducive to agreement.

- **State Your Position Clearly:** Use *claridad* [kla•ree•DAHD] (clarity) and *concisión* [kon•SEE•soh] (conciseness) to present your case without ambiguity.

- **Listen Actively:** Showing that you value the other party's input by asking for their opinion (*¿Cuál es tu opinión?* [KWAL es too oh•pee•NYON]) fosters a collaborative atmosphere.

- **Be Respectful:** Always approach negotiations with respeto [res•PEH•toh] (respect), acknowledging the validity of the other party's perspectives.

These strategies and phrases can enhance your ability to negotiate and persuade effectively within Spanish-speaking contexts, paving the way for more fruitful outcomes.

Phrases for Persuasive Arguments

Persuasion is an art, and every artist has their favorite tools. In your case, it's words. Phrases like *"Te beneficiaría considerar..."* (You would benefit from considering...) or *"Imagina el impacto de..."* (Imagine the impact of...) help paint a picture, making your proposal heard and felt.

Phrasebook

Here's a handy list of persuasive phrases categorized by intent (e.g., to inspire, to reassure, to challenge). Keep it as a reference to spice up your arguments.

1. *Te beneficiaría considerar...* [te bene•fi•sja•REEA kon•si•de•RAR...] — (You would benefit from considering...)
2. *Imagina el impacto de...* [i•ma•HEE•na el im•PAK•to de] — (Imagine the impact of...)
3. *Esto podría significar...* [ES•to po•DREE•a sig•ni•fi•KAR] — (This could mean...)
4. *Considera las ventajas de...* [kon•si•de•RAR las ven•TA•has de...] — (Consider the advantages of...)

5. *¿Has pensado en...?* [as pen•SAH•do en...] — (Have you thought about...?)

6. *Esto ofrece una solución a...* [ES•to o•FRE•se oo•na so•lu•SJON a] — (This offers a solution to...)

7. *Estamos comprometidos con...* [es•TAH•mos kom•pro•me•TEE•dos kon...] — (We are committed to...)

8. *Esta opción supera a las demás porque...* [ES•ta op•SJON su•PE•ra a las de•MAS por•KE] — (This option surpasses the others because...)

9. *Garantiza resultados positivos* [ga•ran•TEE•sa re•sul•TA•dos po•si•TEE•vos] — (It guarantees positive results)

10. *Tu apoyo es crucial para...* [tu a•PO•yo es kru•SJAL PA•ra] — (Your support is crucial for...)

Using these phrases in your arguments can make them more compelling and persuasive, enabling you to convey your ideas and proposals effectively.

Understanding Cultural Nuances in Negotiation

When learning a language, understanding context is as important as learning vocabulary and grammar. In some places, directness signals honesty and strength. In others, it's about weaving subtlety and respect into your requests, acknowledging hierarchy and tradition. For instance, using *"podría"* (could) instead of *"puedo"* (I can) softens requests, making them more palatable.

- **Cultural Quick Tips:** An infographic highlighting key negotiation behaviors in Spanish-speaking countries. A quick glance can save you from a faux pas.

Who you're negotiating with also shapes the dialogue. A young tech entrepreneur might appreciate innovative ideas and bold pitches, while a seasoned executive might value tradition and proven methods. Tailor your approach to your audience.

Practical Exercises for Negotiation

Practice makes perfect, and what better way to hone your skills than by simulating real-life scenarios? Role-play exercises with partners can recreate negotiations ranging from salary discussions to vendor contracts. Switch roles, explore different outcomes, and reflect on best tactics.

- Role-play scenarios are a set of everyday negotiation situations for practice. They include objectives, roles, and debrief questions to enhance learning from each simulation.

Try keeping a negotiation journal. After each real-life negotiation attempt, jot down what happened, what went well, and what could have been better. Reflecting on these experiences sharpens your instincts for next time.

Negotiation and persuasion are not just about getting what you want; they're about creating relationships where everyone feels valued and heard. With proper preparation, phrases, and understanding of cultural nuances, you can navigate these waters confidently and gracefully. Whether clinching a deal, influencing a decision, or choosing where to dine, your newfound skills will open doors and build bridges, making every interaction a stepping stone to success.

This journal entry is a practical example for a Spanish learning student on thoughtfully approaching negotiation scenarios.

Keeping such records encourages active reflection and continuous improvement in language proficiency and negotiation skills.

Negotiation Journal Example for a New Spanish Learning Student

Date: September 20, 2024

Scenario: Salary Negotiation with Manager

Objective: To negotiate a 10% salary increase based on my performance and the completion of key projects.

Preparation:

- I have reviewed my achievements and how they contributed to the company's goals.

- Practiced phrases like *"Creo que mi contribución a los proyectos recientes justifica..."* (I believe my contribution to recent projects justifies...) and *"¿Cómo podemos llegar a un acuerdo sobre mi salario?"* (How can we reach an agreement on my salary?).

What Happened: I started the conversation by expressing gratitude for the opportunity to discuss my role and its impact on the company. I then presented my case, highlighting specific achievements and how they aligned with our team's objectives. I used the phrase *"Apreciaría su apoyo para reconocer mi contribución con un ajuste salarial."* (I would appreciate your support in recognizing my contribution with a salary adjustment.)

What Went Well:

- My manager appreciated my preparation and the clarity with which I presented my achievements.
- Using Spanish phrases confidently helped me to convey my points more persuasively.
- The manager agreed to revisit my salary, acknowledging my contributions.

Areas for Improvement:

- I could have been more assertive in stating my desired salary increase.
- I need to practice negotiating terms more fluidly in Spanish to build confidence.

Reflection: The negotiation went smoother than I anticipated, likely due to my preparation and the use of specific examples to back up my request. Practicing phrases beforehand was invaluable. However, I'll work on being more direct about my expectations and using more varied vocabulary to express my thoughts and requirements more dynamically.

Debrief Questions:

1. Did I clearly articulate my achievements and their impact?
2. How effectively did I use Spanish to enhance my negotiation?
3. What non-verbal cues could I incorporate to strengthen my position in future negotiations?

Next Steps:

- Review additional vocabulary related to achievements and compensation.
- Role-play more complex negotiation scenarios with language partners.
- Observe and note effective negotiation tactics in real-life situations to incorporate them into my strategy.

Chapter 4.1 Common Spanish Phrases

1. *La preparación para la negociación incluye definir nuestros objetivos.* [lah preh•pah•rah•see•OHN PAH•rah lah neh•goh•see•ah•see•OHN een•KLOO•yeh deh•fee•NEER noo•EHS•trohs o•heh•TEE•vohs] — (Preparation for negotiation includes defining our goals.)

2. *Debemos establecer los límites antes de empezar.* [deh•BEH•mohs ehs•tah•bleh•SEHR lohs LEE•mee•tehs AHN•tehs deh EHM•peh•sahr] — (We must establish the limits before starting.)

3. *Lo que ofrezco es una alternativa innovadora.* [loh keh oh•FREHZ•koh ehs OO•nah ahl•tehr•nah•TEE•vah een•noh•vah•DOH•rah] — (What I'm offering is an innovative alternative.)

4. *¿Cuál es tu opinión sobre esta propuesta?* [KWAHL ehs too oh•pee•NYON SOH•breh EHS•tah proh•PWEHS•tah] — (What is your opinion about this proposal?)

5. *Necesitamos flexibilidad para adaptarnos a los cambios.* [neh•seh•see•TAH•mohs flehk•see•bee•lee•DAHD PAH•rah ah•dap•TAHR•nos ah lohs KAHM•byohs] — (We need flexibility to adapt to changes.)

6. *Es importante que mantengamos la claridad durante todo el proceso.* [ehs eem•por•TAHN•teh keh man•ten•GAH•mohs lah klah•ree•DAHD doo•RAHN•teh TOH•doh el proh•SEH•soh] — (It's important that we maintain clarity throughout the process.)

7. *Asegurémonos de ser concisos en nuestras demandas.*
[ah•seh•goo•REH•moh•nohs deh sehr
kohn•SEE•sohs ehn noo•EHS•trahs
deh•MAHN•dahs] — (Let's make sure to be concise
in our demands.)

8. *Te beneficiaría considerar nuestras alternativas.* [teh
beh•neh•fee•see•ah•REE•ah
kohn•see•deh•RAHR noo•EHS•trahs
ahl•tehr•nah•TEE•vahs] — (You would benefit
from considering our alternatives.)

9. *Imagina el impacto de alcanzar un acuerdo mutuo.*
[ee•mah•HEE•nah el eem•PAHK•toh deh
ahl•KAHN•sahr oon ah•KWER•doh
MOO•too•oh] — (Imagine the impact of reaching a
mutual agreement.)

10. *Esta opción supera a las demás porque garantiza
resultados positivos.* [EHS•tah ohp•see•OHN
soo•PEH•rah ah lahs deh•MAHS POHR•keh
gah•rahn•TEE•sah reh•sool•TAH•dohs
poh•see•TEE•vohs] — (This option surpasses
the others because it guarantees positive
results.)

4.2 Writing in Spanish: Emails, Texts, and Letters

Navigating the landscape of written Spanish offers a unique
set of challenges and rewards akin to piecing together a
puzzle. Each word and punctuation mark plays a crucial role
in conveying your message accurately and effectively.
Whether drafting a formal business email, exchanging
casual texts with friends, or penning heartfelt letters, the key

lies in adapting your writing to suit the occasion and recipient.

Writing for Different Audiences

Adapting your tone and style depending on whom you're writing to is the first step toward effective communication. A business email to a potential client in Madrid might start with a formal *"Estimado Sr. Rodríguez"* and end with *"Atentamente,"* reflecting respect and professionalism. Conversely, a text to a new friend made on your last trip to Chile might open with *"¡Hola!"* and conclude with *"Nos vemos,"* embodying the warmth and friendliness of casual interaction.

- **For Professional Emails:** Use a formal tone, straightforward subject lines, and professional sign-offs. Ensure clarity and brevity, keeping the reader's time in mind.
- **For Casual Texts:** Embrace a relaxed tone, use local slang carefully, and allow your personality to shine through. Emojis can add tone and clarity.
- **For Personal Letters:** Here, you can express emotions more vividly. Use descriptive language to convey feelings and experiences.

KEYWORDS/PHRASES AND HOW TO PRONOUNCE THEM:

For Professional Emails:

1. *Estimado Sr./Sra.* [es•tee•MAH•do se•NYOR/se•NYORA] — (Dear Mr./Mrs.)
2. *Atentamente* [a•ten•ta•MEN•te] — (Sincerely)
3. *Asunto* [ah•SOON•to] — (Subject)
4. *Le agradezco* [leh a•gra•DEZ•co] — (I thank you)
5. *Cordialmente* [cor•DEEAL•men•te] — (Cordially)

For Casual Texts:

1. *¡Hola!* [O•lah] — (Hi!)
2. *Nos vemos* [nos VEH•mos] — (See you)
3. *¿Qué tal?* [KEH tal] — (How's it going?)
4. *Un abrazo* [oon ah•BRA•zo] — (A hug)
5. *Emoji* — (Emoji)
6. Same as in English, but pronounced [e•mo•hi] in Spain

For Personal Letters:

1. *Querido/a* [ke•REE•doh/dah] — (Dear)
2. *Con cariño* [kon ka•REE•nyo] — (With love)
3. *Te extraño* [teh eks•TRA•nyo] — (I miss you)
4. *Recuerdos* [re•KWER•dos] — (Regards)
5. Espero tu respuesta [es•PEH•ro too res•PWES•tah] — (I look forward to your reply)

Structuring Your Written Communication

Understanding the structure of written Spanish is like knowing the rules of the road before driving. Every letter, whether digital or on paper, should have a clear beginning, middle, and end.

- **Greetings and Introductions:** Start with an appropriate greeting. The opening sentence should state the purpose of your letter or email and set the tone.
- **Body Content:** This is where you dive into the details. Keep paragraphs focused and organized, whether you're making a request, providing information, or sharing news.
- **Sign-offs:** Conclude with a closing that matches the tone of your message. *"Cordialmente"* suits formal letters, while *"Un abrazo"* is perfect for friends.

Aim for coherence and cohesion, ensuring your ideas flow logically from one to the next, and utilize transitional phrases to guide your reader through your message.

KEYWORDS/PHRASES AND HOW TO PRONOUNCE THEM:

Greetings and Introductions

- *Estimado Sr./Sra.* [es•tee•MAH•do se•NYOR/se•NYORA] — (Dear Mr./Mrs.)
- *Hola* [O•lah] — (Hello)

Body Content

- *Quisiera informarle* [kee•SYE•ra een•for•MAR•leh] — (I would like to inform you)
- *Tengo una solicitud* [TEN•goh OO•na so•lee•see•TUD] — (I have a request)
- *Adjunto encontrará* [ad•HOON•to en•kon•tra•RAH] — (Attached you will find)

Sign-offs

- *Cordialmente* [kor•dee•AL•men•te] — (Cordially)
- *Un abrazo* [oon a•BRAH•soh] — (A hug)

Transitional Phrases

- *Además* [ah•de•MAS] — (Furthermore)
- *Por lo tanto* [por lo TAN•to] — (Therefore)
- *En conclusión* [en kon•kloo•see•ON] — (In conclusion)

Coherence and Cohesion

- *En primer lugar* [en pree•MER loo•GAR] — (In the first place)
- *Para concluir* [PAH•rah kon•klu•EER] — (To conclude)
- *Finalmente* [fee•nal•MEN•te] — (Finally)

Common Writing Pitfalls to Avoid

Mistakes in written communication can range from amusing to costly, especially in a professional context. Awareness of common pitfalls is the first defense against them.

- **False Cognates:** Words like *"embarazada"* (pregnant) and "embarassed" can lead to unintended meanings. Always double-check cognates and their actual meanings in Spanish.
- **Verb Tense Mistakes:** Spanish verb tenses can be tricky. Pay special attention to using past tenses— *"pretérito"* and *"imperfecto"*—to ensure you convey the correct timing of actions.
- **Inappropriate Register Use:** Using overly casual language in a formal email or vice versa can send the wrong message. Match your register to the context and relationship.
- **Typos and Grammatical Errors:** These can undermine your credibility. Use spell-check tools and, if possible, have a native speaker review essential documents.

Familiarizing yourself with these common errors and taking steps to avoid them can significantly enhance the clarity and professionalism of your written Spanish.

Awareness of these false cognates can help beginner Spanish learners avoid common written and spoken communication errors.

1. *Embarazada*

- **Meaning:** Pregnant
- **False Friend:** Embarrassed
- **Pronunciation:** [em•ba•ra•SA•da]

2. *Actual*

- **Meaning:** Current
- **False Friend:** Actual
- **Pronunciation:** [ak•TWAL]

3. *Asistir*

- **Meaning:** To attend
- **False Friend:** To assist
- **Pronunciation:** [a•sis•TEER]

4. *Carpeta*

- **Meaning:** Folder
- **False Friend:** Carpet
- **Pronunciation:** [kar•PE•ta]

5. *Constipado*

- **Meaning:** Cold (as in the illness)
- **False Friend:** Constipated
- **Pronunciation:** [kons•ti•PA•do]

6. *Éxito*

- **Meaning:** Success
- **False Friend:** Exit
- **Pronunciation:** [EK•see•to]

7. *Fábrica*

- **Meaning:** Factory
- **False Friend:** Fabric
- **Pronunciation:** [FA•bree•ka]

8. *Librería*

- **Meaning:** Bookstore
- **False Friend:** Library
- **Pronunciation:** [li•bre•REEA]

9. *Ropa*

- **Meaning:** Clothes
- **False Friend:** Rope
- **Pronunciation:** [ROH•pa]

10. *Sensible*

- **Meaning:** Sensitive
- **False Friend:** Sensible
- **Pronunciation:** [sen•SEE•ble]

Practice Exercises for Writing Skills

Improving your writing skills in Spanish is a process that involves regular practice and feedback. Here are some exercises designed to sharpen your abilities across a range of formats:

- **Email Writing Exercise:** Draft an email requesting information about a service. Focus on structuring your message clearly and using formal language. Swap with a partner for feedback.
- **Texting Scenarios:** Create a series of text exchanges between friends planning a weekend outing. Practice using informal language and text abbreviations common in Spanish.
- **Letter to a Pen Pal:** Write a letter describing a recent personal experience to a pen pal. Use descriptive language to bring your story to life and express emotions.

Each exercise sharpens your ability to communicate effectively in written Spanish and deepens your understanding of cultural nuances, enhancing your proficiency and confidence in the language. Here's a simplified text exchange scenario between two friends, Alex and Sam, planning a weekend outing.

Alex: *¡Hola! ¿Qué planes para este finde?*
[O•la KEH PLA•nes PAH•ra ES•te FEEN•de?]
(Hi! What plans for this weekend?)

Pat: *¡Hola! Nada aún. ¿Quieres hacer algo?*
[O•la NA•da a•OON. KJE•res a•SER AL•go]
(Hi! Nothing yet. Want to do something?)

Alex: *Sí, ¿qué tal si vamos al cine?*
[si KEH tal si VAH•mos al SEE•ne?]
(Yes, how about going to the movies?)

Pat: *Me gusta la idea. ¿Qué película?*
[me GOOS•ta la i•DE•a. ke pe•LEE•ku•la?]
(I like the idea. Which movie?)

Alex: *¿Qué te parece "La Aventura Espacial"?*
[KEH te pa•RE•se la a•ven•TOO•ra es•pa•SJAL?]
(How about "The Space Adventure"?)

Pat: *Genial. ¿A qué hora?*
[he•NJAL a KEH O•ra]
(Great. What time?)

Alex: *A las 7 PM. Nos vemos en el cine.*
[a las SJE•te pe eme. nos VEH•mos en el SI•ne]
(At 7 PM. See you at the movies.)

Pat: *Perfecto. Hasta entonces.*
[per•FEK•to AS•ta en•TON•ses]
(Perfect. Until then.)

Chapter 4.2 Common Spanish Phrases

For Professional Emails:

1. *Estimado Sr./Sra., le agradezco por su rápida respuesta.*
   [es•ti•MA•do se•NYOR/se•NYORA, le
   a•gra•DES•ko por soo RAH•pee•da res•PWES•ta]
   — (Dear Mr./Mrs., I thank you for your quick
   response.)
2. *Adjunto encontrará el informe solicitado.*
   [ad•HOON•to en•kon•tra•RAH el in•FOR•me
   so•lee•SEE•ta•do] — (Attached you will find the
   requested report.)
3. *Por lo tanto, esperamos su colaboración.* [por lo
   TAN•to, es•pe•RAH•mos soo ko•la•bo•ra•SYON]
   — (Therefore, we look forward to your
   collaboration.)

For Casual Texts:

1. *¡Hola! ¿Qué tal tu día?* [O•la! KEH tal too DEE•ah?]
   — (Hi! How's your day going)
2. *Nos vemos el sábado, ¡un abrazo!* [nos VEH•mos el
   SAH•ba•do, oon a•BRA•so] — (See you on
   Saturday, a hug!)
3. *Te extraño mucho, espero verte pronto.* [te
   eks•TRA•nyo MOO•cho, es•PEH•ro VEHR•te
   PROHN•to] — (I miss you a lot, I hope to see you
   soon.)

For Personal Letters:

1. *Querido/a, recuerdo nuestros momentos con cariño.*
   [ke•REE•do/ke•REE•da, re•KWER•do
   noo•EHS•tros mo•MEN•tos kon ka•REE•nyo] —
   (Dear, I remember our moments fondly.)
2. *Espero tu respuesta con ansias.* [es•PEH•ro too
   res•PWES•ta kon AN•sjas] — (I eagerly look
   forward to your reply.)

Coherence and Cohesion:

1. *En primer lugar, quisiera agradecer tu esfuerzo.* [en
   pri•MER lu•GAR, ki•SJE•ra a•gra•de•SER too
   es•FWER•so] — (In the first place, I would like to
   thank you for your effort.)
2. *Para concluir, estamos comprometidos con alcanzar
   nuestros objetivos.* [PAH•ra kon•kloo•EER,
   es•TAH•mos kom•pro•me•TEE•dos kon
   al•kan•SAR noo•EHS•tros ob•heh•TEE•vos] —
   (To conclude, we are committed to achieving our
   goals.)

Keeping the Game Alive

Hola, amazing learners! Now that you have everything you need to start learning Spanish, it's time to pass on your newfound knowledge and show other readers where they can find the same help.

Simply by leaving your honest opinion of this book on Amazon, you'll guide other beginner Spanish learners to a resource that could change their approach to learning Spanish. Your review doesn't just help them; it keeps the cycle of learning vibrant and alive!

I deeply appreciate your help. Our passion for learning thrives when we share our knowledge, and by leaving a review, you're helping to keep that flame burning bright.

Scan the QR code below to leave your review on Amazon:

Thank you for being a part of this journey and for helping spread the joy of learning Spanish. You are not just learning a language; you are becoming part of a larger story.

Muchas gracias y ¡hasta luego!

Austin Fultz

Conclusion

As we close the exciting pages of Book 1, take a moment to bask in the glow of your achievements. You've dipped your toes and fully dived into the deep ocean of the Spanish language, surfacing with precious words and phrases that now dance off your tongue with newfound confidence. Through phonetic guides, you've conquered pronunciations that once seemed like daunting tongue acrobatics. Your journey through Hispanic culture has equipped you with insights to navigate its rich landscapes with the ease of a local.

From the lively dialogues between friends and family to the engaging exercises that tested your skills, each chapter was a step on an incredible voyage of discovery. You've filled in the blanks on worksheets, understanding and appreciating a language and culture spanning continents and hearts.

As you approach this milestone, remember that it is not an endpoint but a gateway. The knowledge you've gained is a solid and proper foundation upon which you will build even greater mastery in **Book 2**. Your adventure in learning Spanish does not pause here—it only gains momentum.

So, as you prepare to turn the page to the next chapter of your learning adventure, remember to carry forward the spirit of curiosity, the joy of discovery, and the laughter that comes from learning not just a language but a way of seeing and experiencing the world.

And always remember, in the great journey of language learning, every mistake is a stitch of wisdom, and every new word a color added to your palette. You've started painting your masterpiece; let's continue this beautiful journey together. Hasta luego, valiente aprendiz del español. The world of the Spanish language is waiting for you with open arms and endless possibilities.

References

- *Using Multimedia Resources - Colorin Colorado* https://www.colorincolorado.org/using-multimedia-resources#:
- *Spanish Greetings | How to Engage in Meaningful ... - Preply* https://preply.com/en/blog/spanish-greetings/
- *Spanish Conversation for Beginners: 150+ Phrases to ...* https://www.fluentu.com/blog/spanish/spanish-conversation-for-beginners/
- *21 Spanish Speaking Countries. Ultimate Guide With Maps* https://effortlessconversations.com/learn-spanish/spanish-speaking-countries/
- *A Year of Celebrations in Spanish-Speaking Countries* https://www.spanishdict.com/guide/a-year-of-celebrations-in-spanish-speaking-countries
- *The Most Powerful Latin Players in Film, TV and Music* https://www.hollywoodreporter.com/lists/most-powerful-latino-celebrities-executives-hollywood-2023/
- *Hispanic Food: A mouthwatering tour of the 20 best Hispanic dishes from each country* https://baselang.com/blog/travel/hispanic-dishes/
- *The Role of Soccer in Latin American Culture* https://sites.duke.edu/wcwp/2015/02/06/the-role-of-soccer-in-latin-american-culture/
- *The 10 Best Ways to Learn Spanish Vocabulary (Tried-and ...* https://www.fluentu.com/blog/spanish/learn-spanish-vocabulary/
- *300+ Spanish Slang Words from Around the World* https://www.fluentu.com/blog/spanish/spanish-slang/
- *Business Culture and Etiquette in Spain* https://www.todaytranslations.com/consultancy-services/business-culture-and-etiquette/doing-business-in-spain/
- *5 Simple Tips for Overcoming Language Barriers While ...* https://www.gooverseas.com/blog/tips-overcoming-language-barriers-while-traveling
- *20 Useful Phrases for Business Negotiations in Spanish* https://www.livelingua.com/blog/top-business-phrases-in-spanish/
- *210+ Common Spanish Words and Phrases to Build Your ...* https://www.fluentu.com/blog/spanish/common-spanish-words/

- *undefined* undefined
- *Spanish Slang Words: 159 of the Best | Mexican, Cuban & ...* https://www.berlitz.com/blog/spanish-slang
- *10 Spanish Role-Playing Scenarios to Use in Your Classroom* https://www.spanish.academy/blog/10-spanish-role-playing-scenarios-to-use-in-your-classroom/
- *8 benefits of having a language exchange partner* https://www.vivalanguageservices.co.uk/blog/8-benefits-of-having-a-language-exchange-partner/
- *How To Plan A Spanish Language Trip* https://expanish.com/blog/spanish-language-trip/
- *Spain's Greatest Hits: the Recipes to Make Now* https://www.foodandwine.com/travel/classic-spanish-recipes
- *The Power of Mnemonics in Language Learning - WordTap* https://wordtap.net/the-power-of-mnemonics-in-language-learning/
- *17 Smart Spanish Flashcard Apps for Powering Through Vocabulary and Grammar* https://www.fluentu.com/blog/spanish/spanish-flashcard-apps-review/
- *World's Most Complete Spanish Pronunciation Guide ...* https://www.spanish.academy/blog/a-complete-spanish-pronunciation-guide-for-beginners/
- *Benefits of learning Spanish through music - Gengo* https://gengo.com/language-and-culture/spanish-language-day-benefits-learning-spanish-music/#:
- *11 Best Apps to Learn Spanish in 2023 [+Infographics]* https://letsspeakspanish.com/blog/learn-spanish-apps/
- *The Top 5 Benefits of Gamification in Learning* https://www.learnlight.com/en/articles/5-benefits-of-gamification-in-learning/
- *5 Spanish Podcasts for Beginners: Train Your Ear to Native ...* https://www.spanish.academy/blog/five-spanish-podcasts-for-beginners/
- *7 Top VR Language Learning Apps in 2023* https://www.fluentu.com/blog/vr-language-learning/
- *7 Types of Spanish Transition Phrases to Win Any Argument* https://www.realfastspanish.com/vocabulary/spanish-transition-phrases
- *Advanced Certificate in Creative Writing in Spanish* https://as.nyu.edu/departments/spanish/graduate/advanced-certificate-in-creative-writing-in-spanish.html
- *Business Spanish Vocabulary: The Complete Guide (with 70+ ...* https://www.fluentu.com/blog/spanish/business-spanish-vocabulary/

- *12 Proven Methods For Reading Better In Spanish* https://www.
  spanish.academy/blog/12-proven-methods-for-reading-better-in-
  spanish/

Made in United States
Orlando, FL
11 November 2024

53703076R10178